FIFTIES
SOURCE
BOOK

FIFTIES
SOURCE
BOOK

CHRISTOPHER PEARCE

Grange
BOOKS

A QUANTUM BOOK

Published by Grange Books
an imprint of Grange Books Plc
The Grange
Kingsnorth Industrial Estate
Hoo, nr. Rochester
Kent ME3 9ND

1-84013-093-8

QUM5OS

This book is produced by
Quantum Books Ltd
6 Blundell Street
London N7 9BH

Printed in Singapore by Star Standard Industries Pte. Ltd

CONTENTS

CONTENTS

FOREWORD

The fifties, as a decade, was unique - for me it was what was left over from the mid thirties and forties. Teenagers' life was geared to jazz, swing, Bing Crosby, music by Berlin, Porter, Carmichael - the 'pop' music of the time; it was George Raft, Gary Cooper, Betty Grable, the Marx Brothers, W. C. Fields, then 1939, war! When we came out the other end in 1945, we took our forties suits out of moth balls, right, a short back and sides haircut, now back to Benny Goodman, Harry Roy, yes, back to the Palais de Dance - the fox-trot contest - and the wireless of course. Muffet Moppit on AFN, *Midnight in Munich*, the big bands, yes, *Itma* on the light programme and so it was 1939-1945 back again, yes, still using the good old Brylcreem, yes I'm all ready to go back to my trumpet and crooning - it wouldn't be long before I'm in a big band - but, er, it's 1950s now and the big bands aren't around so much and crooning seems to be - well not so much. There's this Charlie Parker, Dizzy Gillespie with Be-Bop, yes ... strange, they're not making many Marx Brothers films, duffle coats were in and I didn't think *Itma* was funny anymore, *Breakfast with Braden* was funny - Max Miller was going out, Max Bygraves was coming in. Then something happened, I met Sellers, Secombe and Bentine - it was a collision of pent-up comic ideas, so music took second place, though I was still faithful to the old 100 Club, Oxford Street. There was 'Humph' and Chris Barber, yes the old jazz still going, but who's this strange bloke Johnny Ray,

Top model, Barbara Goalen, with the Goons, 1954.

and who's this Rock-Around-The-Clock Bill Haley, must say he's different!!!! Why isn't Ambrose on the radio any more ... It's 1956 and the Goons are famous. I didn't know that some lads called the Quarry Men were listening in - times they were a-changing. In conclusion I'd say the fifties was the platform for the sixties.

Spike Milligan

INTRODUCTION

YOU – reflecting this 'Love-Pat' radiance . . . always!

Loose powder turns orange-y . . . dries your skin, too!
But not 'Love-Pat' . . . the complete make up!

If you fear dry skin, *why use loose powder?* Powder dries, soaks up precious skin oils. But 'Love-Pat' *won't* dry your skin. Why? Because it contains up to *3 times as much beauty oil* as loose powder or other compact make-ups. (And that's why it won't turn orange-y either!)

With 'Love-Pat', you smooth on a creamy foundation that has powder's *velvet* finish. To start the day . . . and for touch-ups all day . . . get 'Love-Pat'. Tomorrow!

In 8 skin-matching shades!
Love-Pat De Luxe. 9/6
Love-Pat Refill 5/6
Special Refill. 4/9

Revlon
'LOVE-PAT'
PRESSED POWDER PLUS FOUNDATION WITH LANOLITE

51

NOVEMBER, 1958

To attempt to define a cohesive fifties style is, in many ways, a self-defeating task. Shark-style car fins casting long shadows across a landscape piled with the greatest number of mass-produced items the world had ever seen may appear as the dominant image of the decade, but equally strong are the themes of purist design and technology. The paradoxes are there at every turn: it was the rock-and-roll age that was shared with that of the beat poet; it was the television age during which more people than ever before took up hobbies and leisure pursuits; and it was the age when consumers were persuaded that lifestyle could be bought on instalment plans and when, according to British Prime Minister Harold Macmillan, they had 'never had it so good'. Yet it was also a time when consumers were collectively insecure enough to accept the marketing premise of planned obsolescence, with its relentless onslaught of novelty. This insecurity, although examined by Jules Feiffer, Mort Sahl and Vance Packard, was, on the whole, well disguised by the apparent harmony of a contented consumer society. People were superficially happy to live like grown-up Barbie Dolls. They were prepared to discard a perfectly good year-old Frigidaire in favour of the latest two-tone model, not only because they could afford to do so but also because it was the tempo of the age - with its latest de luxe features, it just had to be better.

CONSUMERISM AND TELEVISION

For most of the fifties, this pattern of popular consumerism was largely an American phenomenon, simply because the United States had the money and manufacturing productivity to make it possible. Nevertheless, other countries experienced the trend vicariously, but through the medium that was the dominant marketing machine of the age - television - and while American audiences were directly targeted by manufacturers through sponsored shows and advertising breaks, exported programmes no less surely sold the American way of life abroad. The imagery of British artist Richard Hamilton's 1956 painting *Just What is it that Makes Today's Homes so Different, so Appealing?* is definitely American.

Conspicuous consumerism was not only the foundation of mass production, it was also the main weapon in the Cold

1. *Cosmetics became a major industry. Life magazine estimated that sales of lipstick to teenagers were worth 20 million dollars during the decade. Ever changing fashions in cosmetic colours served the same purpose as planned obsolescence in the automobile industry.*

2. *The middle class family, often living in suburbs or new towns, became the main target of marketing strategy. Both Richard Nixon in his Moscow speech and Harold Macmillan in his 'You've never had it so good' speech drew attention to their new affluence.*

1

1. The fascination with science and technology was a love-hate relationship. Technological progress was welcome, the sinister side of space became the theme of countless sci-fi horror movies, usually featuring attempts to take over the world. In Invasion of the Saucer Men, an alien injects alcohol into human beings with his claws making them drunk or killing them with overdose.

2. This photograph taken by a United States coastguard in 1952 is typical of many pictures of UFO sightings - its source impeccable, the 'saucers' plausible but unproven.

War. By the time of his notorious 'kitchen' confrontation with Kruschev, Richard Nixon could point to an American refrigerator as a symbol of western society.

FEAR OF THE UNKNOWN
Yet this was not necessarily a reassuring image, for during the fifties the Soviet Union had not only pursued the arms race at a pace that ensured that the decade was lived under the shadow of the bomb, but it had also beaten America into space in 1957 with its sputniks. The polarisation between the lifestyles and ideologies of the Communist bloc countries and the West proved to be a *leitmotif* of the decade. It is now suggested, for instance, that the fear of the unknown (that is, Communism) was transmuted into threats from outer space and a mass of UFO sightings. In turn, these were transformed into the plots of countless B movies. Similarly the imagery of that one great sublimated fear, the atom bomb, became trivialised into a design motif, a *memento mori* appearing on headscarves and picnic trays and embodied as a symbol of peace in the main pavilion of the 1958 Brussels Exposition. At the same time, bomb shelters evolved from being a basic civil defence requirement into a chic accessory for the modern home.

CONSUMERISM AND DESIGN
The major design achievements of the decade were in the production of non-elitist object. The impetus towards this was threefold: first was the need to fuel the output of mass production and its corollary, planned obsolescence; second, consumers came to expect constant stimulus and progress; and finally new materials, particularly plastics and man-made fibres, proliferated. Such was the extent of this growth towards mass production that in 1951 the Herman Miller Co. could provide furniture designed by Charles Eames and George Miller for about half the price of conventional

3. The rocket had been developed towards the end of World War II as the obvious weapon of the future as well as the key to the conquest of space (by the beginning of the decade this was already seen as attainable). Rocket imagery, in the Oldsmobile Rocket series or as a styling device for vacuum cleaners and thermos flasks, became popular. Seen here is the 1952 United States 'Redstone' rocket which had a range of two hundred miles.

4. The Herman Miller Company was uniquely responsible for popularising progressive American furniture design, using major designers and sophisticated manufacturing techniques to produce affordable and non-elitist furniture. Many of its designs are now seen as classics and some, such as this 1954 Eames sofa, are still in production.

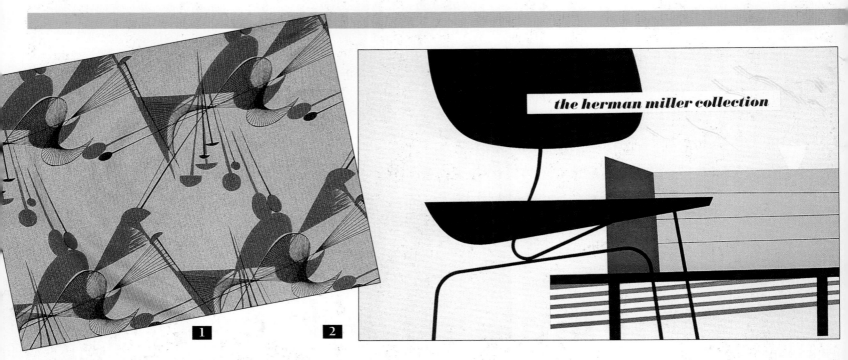

1
2

1. As well as the omnipresent
'cocktail cherry' motif this textile
design uses the spiralling forms
which appeared in furniture and
lighting, the 'snail' of the
Guggenheim museum and
Saarinen's parabolic roof
structures.

2. The Herman Miller Company
is synonymous with post-war
design, applying the techniques of
mass production, hitherto
associated only with cheap
furniture, whilst championing
modernism.

constructions, with a moulded Eames chair selling for $35.

A cross-section of consumer goods, from automobiles through to Coca-Cola dispensers, embodied the work of some of the greatest designers of the age, but the great surge in mainstream popularisation meant that fad styling was everywhere evident - Jackson Pollock's paintings, for example, became the inspiration for countless tacky plastic tabletops and coffee-shop drapes. This parasitic plundering of easily assimilated forms and motifs led to the worst excesses of fifties 'design'. Although this sort of debased copying had been commonplace since the days of the 18th-century cabinet makers, it is more noticeably incongruous when, for example, the anonymous manufacturers of cheap upholstered furniture update it by putting it on tapered, spindly legs, the visual equivalent of the middle-of-the-road musicians who were hauled into recording studios to emulate the new rock-and-roll sounds.

The need for novelty was fuelled by a universal feeling of newness. Of necessity, more people were living in newly built homes than ever before. World War II had devastated most European cities, and some British people found that even the pre-fabricated concrete buildings put up as temporary housing were superior to the Victorian slums destroyed by the Blitz. The functional, well-made Utility furniture was produced by designer Gordon Russell under the supervision of the British government to conserve scarce materials, and this was many people's first experience of new, let alone modern, furniture.

Similarly in the United States, the break-up of many inner-city communities that had taken place in the war, combined with the re-appraisal of housing stock that took place in the immediate post-war period, resulted in the building of the new suburbias, all of which gave a fresh opportunity for at least superficially new lifestyles.

COLLISION OF CULTURES

The political and social changes occasioned by World War II were mirrored in the cross-fertilisation of design and style that took place throughout the late 1940s and the 1950s. Although the overall effect in both the popular and the fine arts, and in industrial design and lifestyle generally, was towards 'Americanism', there were strong influences from many other sources, including Japanese aesthetics; the fulfilment of much of the work of refugees from the pre-war Bauhaus, particularly in architecture; the unique fusion of extrovert chic and elegance that characterised Italian design; and the techniques and subject matter of European cinema. The juxtaposition of different cultures sometimes produced strange results. In the United States, for example, the televised coverage of the Coronation of Queen Elizabeth II was interspersed with advertising breaks, and the event featured the bizarre sight of the Queen stepping out of her coach and being apparently transformed into Miss Pontiac of 1953 emerging from her car - 'Body by Fisher'!

Nevertheless, the fifties are characterised more by the merging of cultures than by the differences between them; the common bond was the growth of consumerism.

In Europe, consumerism was inherent in the work of post-war regeneration. Not only was money injected into industry through the $17 billion of Truman's Marshall Plan, but American industrial designers became active in assisting production and at the same time publicised and promoted

3

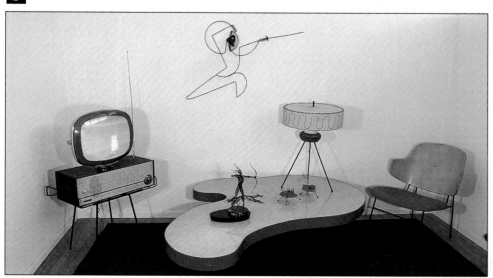

4

3. Levittown, Pennsylvania. The builder William Levitt was responsible for such vast suburban developments, building one hundred and fifty houses a day, so that his name became a generic term for suburbia. These new communities developed their own conventions, satirised by contemporary commentators; in particular the suburbs were ideal environments for the 'keeping up with the Joneses' school of consumerism.

4. The Philco Predicta television of 1958 on the left epitomises the high standard of technical achievement and industrial design that flourished in the United States. The coffee table design is based on the popular artist's palette shape.

1. Then as now the American automobile was seen as a symbol of the age. Its flamboyant excess embodied the creed of conspicuous consumerism. Fittingly its style died with the decade.

2. Now better dressed, with their own identifiable style, these young Britons were enjoying a brief respite before National Service channelled them into the narrow confines of British society.

man against nature, with the conquest of Everest and the Kon-Tiki expedition. Sightings of flying saucers seemed to herald the arrival of visitors from outer space, and both the United States and the Soviet Union had massive space projects. Nuclear power became a reality, with power stations and the nuclear-powered submarines. Jet travel, the miniaturisation of electronics, the early stages of robotics and computers all took place during the decade whose achievements and failures are still directly affecting our lives today.

European design in the United States. Nevertheless, the contrast between the relative poverty of Europe and the apparent affluence of the United States meant that the pace was set by the United States. For example, US refrigerators were of a vastness that could represent in Britain, where food rationing was still in effect, not a week's supply of groceries, but several months', and car ownership in the United States was almost universal at a time when the average European blue-collar worker still cycled to work and regarded the car as a luxury.

Similarly, the United States, which had dominated the popular areas of music and cinema since the beginning of the century, witnessed the birth of two new fifties phenomena, the cult of the teenager, and, of course, rock-and-roll. Teenage emancipation had first become apparent during the war years in the guise of the bobby-soxer, and although in the fifties it was often cynically exploited as nothing more than a new field for consumerism, it was nevertheless part of a general trend towards greater liberalism. The cult of the individual, as a beat poet, as a 'rebel without a cause', or as an angry young man became symbolised by the rock singer, who, armed with new technology in the form of the solid electric guitar, took on a new role and challenged the hierarchy of established order.

Not that the fifties saw the end of class, or racial, or generation, or sexual discrimination, but awareness of these social problems greatly increased. Largely as a result of the consumer boom, there was a general democratising of lifestyle, for mass production, by definition, has to result in a collective aesthetic. Economics do not allow for an elitist refrigerator, and, in any event, today's luxury features become standard on next year's model. Speed of change, or progress, was the spirit of the age, and this, more than anything, appeared to be the fulfilment of the dreams and aspirations of the 20th century. There was the romance of

3. Eddie Cochran outlived the decade by a mere four months, his accidental death in keeping with the 'live fast, die young' image of rock-and-roll.

4. West Side Story, *one of the fifties' most successful stage musicals, enjoyed a revival when it appeared as a film in 1961. Based on Shakespeare's* Romeo and Juliet, *it had pretensions to art. Modern choreography gave a stylish portrayal of a street gang to the dismay of many politicians, police and youth workers. With their own tribal language, laws and conventions the gangs were responsible for much city violence. In 1956 New York teen gangs were estimated to have doubled their use of dangerous weapons over the previous year, with gang murders up 25%.*

3

4

Designed for London Transport in 1954 by Douglas Scott and Eric Ottoway, the Routemaster bus is regarded as a classic in public transport.

CHAPTER ONE
BLUE SKIES
DESIGN

'NEW PRODUCTS WILL APPEAR WHICH WILL MAKE THE FANCIFUL PREDICTIONS THAT
DECORATE OUR ADVERTISING PAGES SEEM COMMONPLACE.'

WALTER DORWIN TEAGUE, NEW YORK TIMES, 1945

INTRODUCTION

During the war years there was a popular belief that when peace returned, the new age would be brighter and better. These morale-boosting visions of the future, which Raymond Loewy called 'Blue Skies Design', created an atmosphere of anticipation, particularly in the United States, where the consumer's expectations were so high that it was politically and economically essential that these dreams did come true. Moreover, because many of the war-time visions of the future had been wildly optimistic, designers found that instead of the usual struggle to get manufacturers and consumers to accept new ideas, it was now a question of being able to fulfill the dreams. Loewy was aware of the dangers. As early as 1943 he wrote: 'Every writer with an extra sheet of paper in his typewriter has dashed off a tale of the 'dream world of the future' more because he knew that such a story would make good reading than because it bears any relation to fact.'

In the event, the fifties saw the realisation of jet and hovercraft travel, the beginning of the Space Age with the launch of Russia's sputniks, atomic power and the first nuclear-powered submarines. The preconditioning of the public's expectations certainly assisted the acceptance of modern architecture as well as of new materials. Plastic, for instance, was freed from its earlier image as a 'substitute' material, and by 1956 the Goodrich Company could show a House of Today, in which plastic was used in a hundred different ways, from the roof to the kitchen sink. The

1. The station wagon, often a second car, became almost symbolic of the new American lifestyle, conjuring up images of the family outing.

designer, rather than the scientist, was seen as the key to the new age. Indeed, since the development of the atom bomb, scientists had become seen as somewhat sinister figures, while designers often became publicly known, even cultish. Sometimes this was used to endorse a product in advertising. In 1950 Frigidaire cookers, for example, were advertised as having been designed by Raymond Loewy, and in 1957 the United Jukebox similarly stressed Loewy's design role.

The use of identified designers as selling points humanised what might otherwise be regarded as the results of remote mass production and replaced, by association, the individual craftsman who was all but extinct. Popular magazines found design newsworthy, and public interest meant that projects such as the 'Useful Objects' exhibitions at New York's Museum of Modern Art, the 'Ideas for Better Living' exhibition at the Walker Arts Centre Everyday Art Gallery (1946), which featured designs for a solar house, and Marcel Breuer's house at the Museum of Modern Art (1949), reached the end user rather than just the designer.

EUROPE IN AMERICA

Awareness of design did much to break down chauvinist attitudes to foreign influence. Although the United States dominated *the* fifties as the consumer society, America was receptive to the influences of Europe, the East and Scandinavia. For instance, although some Scandinavian design had been seen in the 1940s, most notably in Georg Jensen's New York store, in 1950 Swedish Modern Inc. began the large-scale importation of Swedish goods, and English, French, Czechoslovakian, Italian and German designs were all being exhibited in the United States by 1950. The 1949 exhibition of German goods at the Museum of Science and Industry was organised because both the State Department and the US Army considered it essential that the German economy be rebuilt. In April 1949, with singular lack of foresight, *Interiors* magazine commented: 'no one even dreams that German designs will compete with our mass-produced articles.' One item on show was the Volkswagen beetle. Less than ten years later, in 1958, *Life* ran an article headed 'Volkswagen, Go Home!' about the threat to the American car industry from foreign competition. Japan was also represented in the United States, the Japanese Trade Centre opening in 1954.

Similarly, American design was exhibited around the world, and American designers were active in the rebuilding of industry and industrial products in Europe and Japan. The United States had not exhibited before the war as it was felt that US designs were too influenced by Europe to satisfy the criterion of originality. But at the tenth Italian Triennale in 1954, the second since the war, the United States exhibited some 40 items, including an outboard motor (Brook Stevens), a power tool (Peter Müller-Munk), a food

1

Cold War, and although the export of American goods was, at that time, not particularly important to the country's economy, the propaganda value of examples of the 'American way of life' was. The consumer item as a symbol reached its climax in 1959 when, in a surprising thaw in the Cold War, America and the Soviet Union agreed to exchange exhibitions. Public reaction was mixed. Some were apprehensive that, after Russia's space coup with the sputnik, there might be other surprises. Luxury air-conditioned limousines? Fully automatic kitchens? As it was, the Russian exhibition was of the low standard that most Americans had assumed it would be. In turn, Vice President Richard Nixon, opening the Moscow exhibition, televised by both Russia and America, recited the roll-call of consumerism - 44 million families, three quarters of them home owners, owning 56 million cars, 50 million television sets and 153 million radios; all combining to form what he described as 'the ideal of prosperity for all in a classless society'.

But later Nixon did a most extraordinary thing. He and

2. Having been synonymous with 'the American way of life' throughout the forties, the early fifties Wurlitzer juke box was a compromise between its glamorous image and old-fashioned technology, and the new 'clean' look.

3. General Motors, which also built locomotives, built the 'train of tomorrow' in 1947 as a design exercise. Especially innovative was the glass Astra Dome observation car, an idea adopted by other manufacturers such as Union Pacific, whose Domeliner was advertised by Ronald Reagan.

2

3

mixer (Francesco Collura), plastic dinner ware (Russel Wright) and a bathroom scale (Raymond Loewy). The exhibition catalogue gave further recognition to American designers by acknowledging that it was they who had invented the term Industrial Design.

BUILT-IN OBSOLESCENCE

The examples of American design mentioned above are now, of course, accepted as items of everyday life, but in the fifties, as the gap between the expectations of the average American consumer and those of consumers in most other countries widened, it was the more obvious examples of consumerist design that became synonymous with 'Americanism'. By the mid-fifties conspicuous consumerism, not just consumerism, had become a creed. In an economy geared to constant renewal through planned obsolescence, Americans were told that it was their patriotic duty to spend.

Consumer spending was also an essential weapon in the

Krushchev were visiting the show house, which was a genuine low-budget suburban home actually built in Moscow by a Long Island builder. Standing in the kitchen, Nixon explained the choice of washing machines available. Krushchev commented that choice was not important if the product was good, to which Nixon replied that it was better to be discussing washing machines than rockets. As they left the kitchen area, Krushchev indicated the equipment and commented: 'This is probably always out of order.' Nixon agreed, publicly admitting that the symbolic heart of American consumerism was unreliable. He had to, because by the end of the fifties the quality of American consumer items had fallen, almost in direct proportion to the increase in volume. Now the best designed and most reliable kitchen items were made by Moulinex, Philips, Braun and Zanussi.

SCANDINAVIAN MODERN AND UTILITY

The disenchantment felt by Americans with many of their domestic products reflected a change that had been taking place throughout the decade. The United States was the only major power to have survived the war with its manufacturing capacity not only intact, but actually enhanced. Furthermore, as we have seen, there was a generally shared optimism in a brighter consumer future. Britain, by contrast, faced the immediate post-war period under a Labour government that was committed to 'the establishment of a Socialist Commonwealth of Great Britain'. There was a shortage of consumer items and of raw materials, and most goods, including food and clothing, were rationed. The most dominant design aesthetic was Utility, which was derived from the Scandinavian Modern style that had been popularised at the 1930 Stockholm Exhibition. Scandinavian Modern tempered Modernism with the humanising effect of natural wood, and one of its leading exponents was Sven Markelius, Stockholm's chief architect.

British design, both in architecture and in the industrial designs of such people as Wells Coates, was regarded as akin to German, and Britain had welcomed Bauhaus refugees from Hitler, including Walter Gropius, Marcel Breuer and László Moholy-Nagy. Nevertheless, it was the Scandinavian Modern style, exemplified by the furniture of Gordon Russell, that was to be the 'official' aesthetic of the forties and early fifties. Such had been the loss of housing during the war that the British government, through the Board of Trade, set up a Design Panel, headed by Russell, to oversee the production of furniture that could be made within the restriction of war-time material shortages. This Utility furniture, which was given traditional-sounding names like Cotswold and Chiltern, has been criticised as retrogressive and tainted with the cottage aesthetic of William Morris. It should, however, be remembered that the designs were limited not only by restrictions on the available materials

1

1. 'Poetry in motion' they may have been, but the powerful engines tested in road racing, the styling and the marketing all seemed just a bit pointless as road building programmes were overtaken by Detroit's massive output.

and production facilities, but also because they had to be acceptable to the average public, for many of whom it was their first experience of 'modern' design. Homely as these pieces now seem, many people found them too spartan, and a black market industry for customising Utility furniture was soon flourishing.

The Design Panel was followed in 1944 by the Council of Industrial Design, another government-sponsored body, which staged exhibitions, including 'Britain Can Make It' (1946). The Council was also involved with the design aspects of the Festival of Britain (1951), by which time Scandinavian Modern had become accepted as standard for Modern British. Although the style was later challenged by the New Brutalists - which began with the architecture of Alison and Peter Smithson - and received periodic challenges, including the Smithsons' House of the Future at the 1956 Ideal Home Exhibition, it continued to dominate the fifties and was exemplified in the furniture of Robert Heritage and the ceramics produced by Poole Pottery.

Not only was the 'official' modern aesthetic conservative, however; the nostalgia boom of the early fifties, with its revival of Victorianism that was quite prominent at the Festival of Britain, caused further confusion. The rebuilding of production facilities was slow, and industry, through Government control, was directed at export rather than the home market. The influence of the Bauhaus that had been apparent in pre-war design had been lost to the Scandinavian style, and both Gropius and Moholy-Nagy left for the new design atmosphere in America.

In the rest of Europe the greatest design explosion was taking place in Italy, where designers were freed from the links between Futurism and Fascism that had existed since the 1920s. Not only did Italian design benefit from official American aid (Truman's Marshall Plan injected some $17 billion into rebuilding Europe) but there was a general sympathy in America with Italy. In 1947 a charitable body had led to the opening of the House of Italian Handicrafts in New York, and in 1950, under the auspices of the Art Institute of Chicago, prominent American designers visited Italy to compile an exhibition of design and craft, 'Italy at Work'. It was widely felt that craft design was Italy's strong point; Walter Teague commented in the catalogue: 'I'm no traitor to mass production, which enables Americans as a whole to enjoy far better designed products and many more of them than are available to the mass of Italians, but a designer could not help but be delighted and stimulated by the daring *tours de force* his Italian colleagues could indulge in at will.'

Among those exhibiting were Gio Ponti, Roberto Menghi and Carlo Mollino, Olivetti and Innocenti. The exhibition was the foundation of a new Italian Renaissance, which, together with revived Triennales, made Italy a major design influence in the world.

DESIGN FOR MANUFACTURE

American designers already took a realistic attitude to commercial requirements. Raymond Loewy had written that his concept of aesthetic 'consists of a beautiful sales curve shooting upwards', and it was in the areas of mass consumer design, particularly the automobile, that the dream could become reality. Proved in stock form at races at Nascar and Daytona and in the Mexican Road Race, these cars were, at least during the early fifties, well made and, compared with other nations' products, luxurious.

The efficient American systems of mass production, which had been developing since the days of Henry Ford and had been refined in war-time production, ensured a constant stream of products. However, this required an equally constant consumer demand, which even the growing affluent society could not match. One solution was saturation: the consumer was encouraged to own two cars and several television sets and to indulge in non-stop shopping. In the manner of Blue Skies Design, new always meant better, and to have other than new was settling for second best. Vance Packard quotes house builders calling other than new houses 'used', and thus putting them on the same level as used cars. It was an obvious requirement of this marketing strategy that 'new' had to be identifiably so, and as the pace was faster than genuine design or technical improvements, styling became the main weapon of planned obsolescence.

In 1955 Harley Earl, whose design motto was 'Go all the way and then back off', explained: 'Our big job is to hasten obsolescence. In 1934 the average car ownership span was five years; now it is two years. When it is one year we will

2. The days when Henry Ford could offer a car in 'any colour as long as it's black' were long forgotten when fashion colours added yet another angle to the styling wars. By the end of the decade, few new cars were sold as standard, the majority of buyers choosing at least some of the optional extra features that were offered.

3. Domestic appliances shared with automobiles the distinction of being prime symbols of consumerism. An up-to-date kitchen was seen as the heart of modern living, and although refrigerators lacked the styling opportunities offered by automobiles, the range of colours offered by Westinghouse was extreme, even by the standards of the day.

have a perfect score.' These ideas became embodied in the cars that *Life* described as 'the high-powered dreamboat that looked as if it had been rolled in chromium batter,' or, as Loewy commented, a 'jukebox on wheels'. The same design philosophies were being applied, though sometimes less obviously so, to other consumer goods.

Towards the end of the decade, however, a general disenchantment with the dream, as well as a noticeable deterioration in the quality of goods and the cultural shock of Russia's advanced space technology led to a slowing down of the roller coaster of consumerism. 'There was a heady scent of European perfume in the air,' commented Herbert Bream, in his article 'Volkswagen, Go Home!' In the increased importation of small European cars, Bream saw a greater consumer maturity demanding 'a new kind of styling, one that will not be an obvious badge of wealth and social importance'. The new badge would, in effect, say: 'I am not nouveau riche, I like understatement and efficiency, not flamboyant extravagance. I expect my automobile to look and handle like an automobile, not a jet bomber.' Answering his own question 'Is the small European type car just a fad?', Bream concluded: 'No more a fad than the growing US taste for foreign foods, clothes and decor. American tastes and appreciation are widening in cars as well as in other things.' He neglected, however, to mention that the excesses of Detroit were the products of marketing rather than of design, and that in the immediate post-war period it was America that had been the main sponsor of European design.

1. The concept of 'newness' that characterised the period did much to pave the way for the use of new materials in consumer products. Plastics were no longer expected to imitate natural materials, although artificial silks and plastic crocodile skin became part of the kitsch aesthetic.

2. Raymond Loewy, pictured in 1939 with the Studebaker Champion, had a unique role in promoting the industrial designer as essential not only to the production process but also to marketing. His career encompassed projects as diverse as Coca-Cola and the US space programme.

3. These examples from an exercise in studies of equilibrium from László Moholy-Nagy's preliminary course could at first glance be taken for one of Mies van der Rohe's architectural designs; a graphic demonstration of the influence of the Bauhaus.

4. War production brought about major changes in manufacturing techniques, bringing to almost every industry the concept of production-line assembly that was first developed by Henry Ford. Wartime developments, particularly in electronics and moulded plastics, became assimilated into the consumer boom.

5. Raymond Loewy designed the S-I locomotive in 1937, which introduced the streamlined, aerodynamic lines of the 'modern' train. Designed through the pioneering use of a wind tunnel, the train was capable of speeds in excess of 120 mph.

ON THE ROAD-USA

1. 'Living room' interiors in the 1959 General Motors range typified the luxury image of the era. However, the advertising copy, stressing as it does the longevity of the body and interior, is indicative of the end of the era of the obsolescent car, which had been the industry's goal during the fifties.

2. Contrary to the general trend, Nash, which was part of the Kelvinator (refrigerator) group, produced small, economy cars. The Rambler Country Club of 1951 was remarkable for its convertible landau style, with a roof that folded back to leave the window framework in place. Advertised as the world's safest convertible, it also achieved over 30 miles to the gallon in the Mobilgas Economy Run.

3. In 1953 Ford registered the name Thunderbird, itself the most powerful of the 'image' names. The 'T-Bird' was first launched in 1954, and from subsequent styling changes emerged the definitive 1956 model, seen here. The 'porthole' window visible at the back of the detachable hardtop was favoured by 80 per cent of buyers.

4. Cadillac, which had introduced embryo fins in the forties, was stuck with the styling clichés that characterised the American automobile of the fifties. In this 1959 Coupe De Ville, the fins, bullet lights and acres of chrome had reached their apogee and were replaced by the simpler lines of the next decade.

4

5

6

5. Now something of a cult classic, the 1958 Ford Edsel Citation was, at the time, a commercial flop. The public rejected it, criticising its appearance - 'like an Oldsmobile sucking a lemon' - its handling and even its name.

6. The new suburbs had brought about social changes, and the station wagon came into its own during the 1950s, often as a second car for supermarket shopping. Illustrated is the 1958 Nash Rebel.

7. The distinctive bullet nose of this 1950 Studebaker had first appeared in the Raymond Loewy-designed 1945 Starliner sports car - 'the first American sports car'. Studebaker was closer to the European look than other manufacturers.

7

1. The Jaguar XK120 was introduced in 1948. Famous for its powerful 3½-litre engine, it was joined by a fixed-head version in 1951.

3. The Jaguar XK120C, known as the C-type, was derived from the sports model as a competition car. While the production XK120 was built on an ash frame, the C-type was on a tubular steel framework. In its first year of production, 1951, it won the Le Mans 24-hour Race. Racing success during the fifties made the Jaguar internationally known.

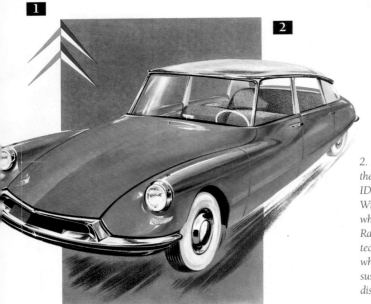

2. Following the DS19 of 1955, the more economical Citroen ID19 was introduced in 1956. With its futuristic body shape, which reveals the influence of Raymond Loewy, and its technical innovations of front-wheel drive and hydro-pneumatic suspension, it is one of the most distinctive designs of the age.

6. The British way with Italian chic. Their woven shopping basket was not a standard feature of the Vespa motor scooter.

4. Destined to become a cult car, the mini, seen here with its designer Alec Issigonis, was introduced in 1959. A 'blank cheque' development programme produced its revolutionary transverse engine design. Produced as an economy car, the first models had spartan interiors, the interior doors being opened by pull cords.

5. The British rock-and-roll singer Tommy Steele, with his car, a Ford Zephyr. Both represent a form of diluted American style. The 1956 Zephyr was the middle of Ford's range; the cheapest was the Consul, a four-cylinder car, while the most expensive, the Zodiac, shared the same six-cylinder engine and bodywork as the Zephyr but had more luxurious fittings.

7. First appearing in the late forties, Italian motor scooters symbolised the high-tech leisure image of the fifties in the same way as espresso coffee machines. The 1953 film Roman Holiday, starring Gregory Peck, Audrey Hepburn and a Vespa scooter, further exposed Italian style to the world. The scooter shown here is a Lambretta.

LIBERATING THE HOUSEWIFE

1. In the United States, the refrigerator was second only to the automobile as an exercise in planned obsolescence, and each year's new models had extra features, different styling and even colour changes. The crown the lady wears, while incongruous, was a common advertising device, used to give an impression of domestic luxury.

2. The electric iron became a symbol of the electric home, itself a phenomenon of the decade as even rural areas became connected to power supplies.

3. Europe was slower than the United States to adopt the fitted kitchen. Apart from the electric iron, this scene demonstrates the continued use of traditional utensils. Although they were available before the fifties, electric vacuum cleaners, food mixers and mincers can be seen as examples of 'new technology'.

4. The designer Dieter Kams (b.1932) brought a new style of minimalist elegance to the electrical consumer products of Braun. Although stereo sound was established by 1959, the date of this unit, the equipment was normally bulky and tended to emphasise gadgetry. The new aesthetics pioneered by Braun won the company a gold medal at the 1957 Milan Triennale.

4

6

5

7

5. The Ericofon telephone, designed by Gosta Thomas in 1954, remains a classic example of the freedom to explore organic forms made possible by new plastic technology.

6. Even at the end of the decade the mangle (clothes wringer) was still a feature of this 1960 washing machine by Radiation, which embodied all the technology of an American Maytag from the 1940s.

7. By the end of the decade the high-tech kitchen had become the universal ideal. Not only were fitted appliances standard, but there were also attempts to conserve floorspace, as can be seen in this eye-level refrigerator by ETZ Frigeco of France.

SPACE AGE TRAVEL

1

2

5. Expectations of futuristic travel were realised with the hovercraft. This is the 1959 SR NI, the first full-size demonstration of the system.

1. The General Motors 'train of tomorrow' (1947) was a full-size prototype incorporating the latest in design technology. Other manufacturers and designers had been invited by G.M. to contribute.

2. The train of tomorrow was to provide the maximum passenger comfort. This is the refreshment bar. The train also featured the 'Astro Dome' observation car.

3

6. America's first satellite, Explorer 1 in 1958, discovered the Earth's radiation belt. The space race between the USA and Russia dominated the latter half of the decade.

3. The Budd Company also produced their version of the observation car, called the 'Vistadome' and designed by Brook Stevens. It had seats for twenty-four passengers.

4. The Budd Company train used the latest in technology, such as this W.C. compartment made of fibreglass from one moulding.

4

5

7. Rocket technology developed during the final stages of World War 2 and was seen as the key to space-age travel. Shown here is the X-1A rocket-powered plane of the early fifties.

8. The vapour trail became a new sight in the skies, a constant reminder that this was the jet age. It became a popular graphic design motif.

NEW SOUNDS, NEW VISION

1

2

1. Television became the centre of many families' leisure time, a phenomenon that many contemporary commentators found alarming.

2. Television sets themselves tended to be conservatively styled. A rare exception was the futuristic, French Teleavia of 1957, which was designed by Philippe Charbonneaux. The metal-bodied set can both swivel and tilt on its 'table' base, which houses the controls. This two-part concept was also seen in the 1956 Italian Phonola television set.

3. Although juke boxes were still mainly a product of the United States, some were being made in Europe. The 1958 British Chantal Meteor was a unique design, and its futuristic looks made it a cult object.

4. The 1958 Sony TR610, though not the first transistor radio, was the first ultra-compact, pocket type.

5. The portable record-player became a favourite teenage accessory: a symbol of emancipation. Parents preferred the combined radio and record-player, often incorporating a cocktail cabinet, or the sophistication of high-fidelity and stereo.

3

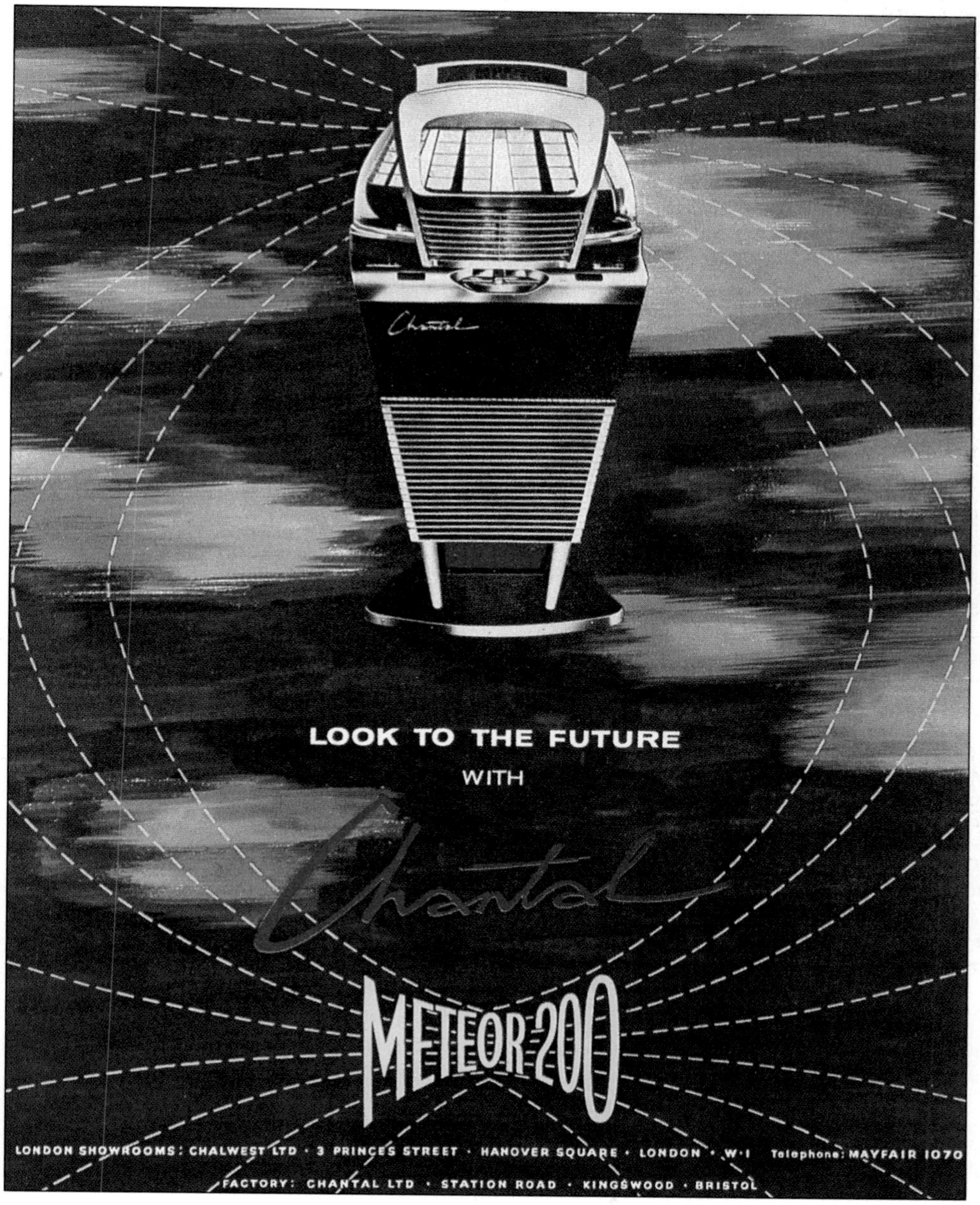

LOOK TO THE FUTURE
WITH
Chantal
METEOR 200
LONDON SHOWROOMS: CHALWEST LTD · 3 PRINCES STREET · HANOVER SQUARE · LONDON · W·1 Telephone: MAYFAIR 1070
FACTORY: CHANTAL LTD · STATION ROAD · KINGSWOOD · BRISTOL

SONY

4

5

THE LEISURE GENERATION

1

2

3

1. The fifties was the first time that leisure and the money to enjoy it became part of nearly everyone's lifestyle. Families in the new suburbs wanted to equip their homes and gardens with all the accessories of a comfortable, up-to-the-minute life. Designers and manufacturers began to gear their products towards women when it was realized how much buying power housewives had.

2. This 1956 photo of record buyers is unusual in that it was taken in East Berlin. These are rock-and-roll or jazz fans. The earphones at the 'music bar' allowed three customers to listen to three separate records without having to go into special listening booths which in this particular shop had been reserved for classical music.

3. Fifties-style affluence - picnicking in the convertible. The number of car owners was growing - Vice President Richard Nixon boasted that the 44 million families in the USA owned 56 million cars. Picknicking became a popular leisure activity - it was also a fine opportunity to use an elaborate coloured picnic set.

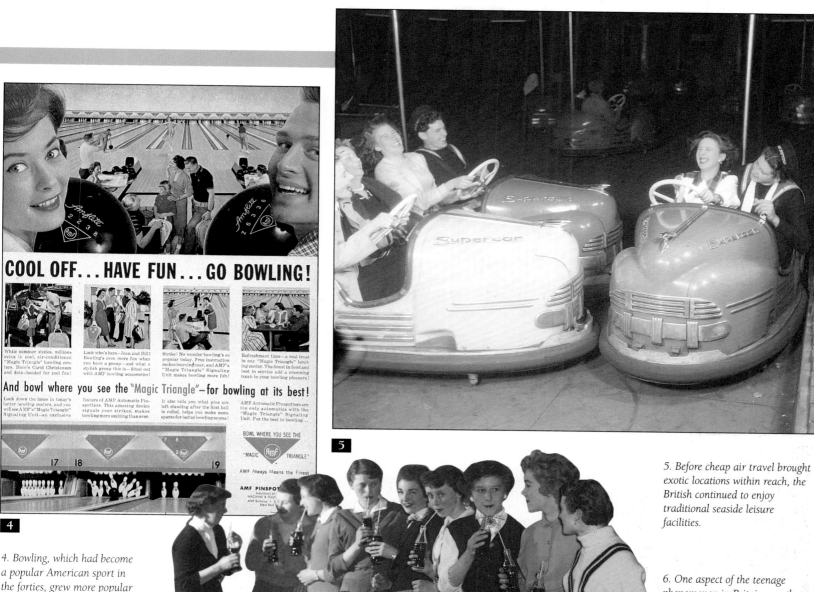

COOL OFF... HAVE FUN... GO BOWLING!

While summer sizzles, millions relax in cool, air-conditioned "Magic Triangle" bowling centers. Here's Carol Christensen and date-headed for cool fun!

Look who's here—Joan and Bill! Bowling's even more fun when you have a group—and what a stylish group *this* is—fitted out with AMF bowling accessories!

Strike! No wonder bowling's so popular today. Free instruction makes learning easy, and AMF's "Magic Triangle" Signaling Unit makes bowling more fun!

Refreshment time—a real treat in any "Magic Triangle" bowling center. The finest in food and best in service add a crowning touch to your bowling pleasure!

And bowl where you see the "Magic Triangle"—for bowling at its best!

Look down the lanes in today's better bowling centers, and you will see AMF's "Magic Triangle" Signaling Unit—an exclusive feature of AMF Automatic Pinspotters. This amazing device signals your strikes, makes bowling more exciting than ever.

It also tells you what pins are left standing after the first ball is rolled, helps you make more spares for better bowling scores!

AMF Automatic Pinspotters are the *only* automatics with the "Magic Triangle" Signaling Unit. For the best in bowling...

BOWL WHERE YOU SEE THE "MAGIC TRIANGLE"

AMF Always Means the Finest

AMF PINSPOTTERS

4

5

4. Bowling, which had become a popular American sport in the forties, grew more popular in the fifties as large-scale bowling alleys were built. It was, for a while, a craze in Britain, prompting the line 'they've changed our local Palais into a bowling alley' in the musical Fings ain't what they used to be.

5. Before cheap air travel brought exotic locations within reach, the British continued to enjoy traditional seaside leisure facilities.

6. One aspect of the teenage phenomenon in Britain was the increase in leisure facilities, such as skating rinks. Any activity that diverted energy from 'delinquency' and rock-and-roll was generally encouraged.

6

37

COFFEE BARS

1. The Italian espresso coffee machine, like the juke box, symbolised high-tech leisure to many British teenagers. The coffee bar, which evolved its own, sometimes off-beat style of decor, became a mecca for youngsters, who, for the first time, were sufficiently affluent to enjoy an independent life-style.

2. By 1958 the British coffee bar was proving a threat to the traditional pub, many of which embarked on modernisation programmes to try to attract young customers.

3. This 1955 shot, by Picture Post photographer Bert Hardy, was part of a photo-journalistic survey of teenage life. The stylized tables and planters are typical.

4. Although by contemporary American standards the 1940 Wurlitzer juke box would have been regarded as antiquated, to these 1955 British teenagers it was an exotic novelty in their less colourful surroundings.

5. An early fifties American lunch counter, later replaced by slicker styles.

The essence of the decade was the musical sensation that swept the world - rock-and-roll.

CHAPTER TWO

THE INCREDIBLE SHRINKING SCREEN

'I GOT SO BUGGED I TURNED IT OFF AND TURNED ON ANOTHER SHOW, BUT THERE WAS THE SAME OLD SHOOT-EM UP AND THE SAME OLD RODEO'

'ALONG CAME JONES' WORDS BY LEIBER AND STOLLER

INTRODUCTION

The fifties have been called the TV Age, and television certainly played an important part in the marketing of products and politics, in entertainment and education and also, as an object itself, at the centre of what might be called TV style. Yet despite the general impression and the expectations of the time, television did not kill the cinema. Many cinemas closed down, it is true, and short films and children's films were made with television in mind, but once the novelty of television wore off, the two media existed side by side, sometimes in competition, more often complementing each other.

Undoubtedly, the most beneficial effect television had on the cinema was the shock it meted out to what had become a complacent industry. It is summed up in the sequence in the film *Sunset Boulevard* (1950) when Joe first sees the faded, reclusive old-time star played by Gloria Swanson. 'I knew you' Joe says. 'You're Norma Desmond, you used to be big!' 'I am big,' she replies. 'It's the pictures that got small.' And she was right. With a few exceptions, Hollywood, its stars and its movies had lost their charisma as the industry grew to rely on a passive audience and hype. 'There's nothing wrong with a bad film that a good box office won't cure,' quipped Groucho Marx.

Now, losing its prime position in the entertainment industry, the cinema fought back by becoming big again, in fact bigger than before. Not in the pre-war larger than life sense, not just physically big, although wide screens and enhanced sound and colour helped, but big in taking on issues and themes that television, with its domestic setting, short attention span and constant disruption by commercial breaks, could not. So Hollywood, which was in the throes of investigation by the Un-American Activities Committee, fought McCarthyism in parables such as *In a Lonely Place* (1950). In a similar manner, it looked at racism in *The Searchers* (1956), *The Defiant Ones* (1958) and *The World, the*

1. The wide screen of CinemaScope, the ideal vehicle for epics, succeeded, both as a novelty and as a genuine improvement in the presentation of films, in bringing audiences back to the cinema.

2. Cinerama, although not an entirely new concept, was the most advanced technique of film presentation mobilised in the attempt to enhance cinema experience and counter the threat posed by television.

3. Audiences at 3-D movies appear to have spent most of the time recoiling in their seats as spears, lions, bullets and fists sprang out of the screen towards them. Once the novelty had worn off, however, the repetition of these effects in otherwise unremarkable films and the need to wear uncomfortable and faintly ridiculous 3-D spectacles hastened the genre's decline.

Flesh and the Devil (1959). The dangers of nuclear power were tackled in the guise of science fiction in *The Incredible Shrinking Man* (1957), *Them!* (1954) and *The Day the Earth Stood Still* (1951), and the darker sides of American life were also explored. Corruption was addressed in *On the Waterfront* (1954), *A Face in the Crowd* (1957), *The Big Heat* (1953), *Executive Suite* (1954), *Sweet Smell of Success* (1957) and humorously, as well as by coincidence topically in the light of the payola scandals of that year, in *The Girl Can't Help It* (1956). The small community, whose image of inherent goodness was almost a sacred cow, was vilified as parochial in *The Wild One* (1954), as spineless in *Shane* (1953) and *High Noon* (1952) or as evil in *Bad Day at Black Rock* (1954).

INVASION OF THE TV WATCHERS

Television itself, however, did not broadcast the non-stop trash that has sometimes been assumed. Part of the reason for television's poor image was simply the indiscriminate viewing the novelty provoked, particularly among children. In an article in *Esquire*, John Crosby reported on a New Jersey school where children were watching television for 31 hours a week to the detriment of their schoolwork. Class results had dropped by 15 per cent. He went on to recount the story of the mother who, afraid of the effect television appeared to be having on her child, consulted a pediatrician: 'Well,' said this learned man bitterly. 'We're rearing a whole generation of morons. You wouldn't want your daughter to be different from the rest, would you? She'd be stoned to death.'

In 1950 there were approximately 7.5 million TV sets in American homes, compared with about 5,000 between RCA's commencing commercial production in 1939 and the end of World War II. There were a hundred TV

stations, broadcasting to 70 cities. The TV sets themselves were manufactured by Philco, General Electric, Capehart (the jukebox company that Farnsworth Television had taken over in 1938), Dumont, Zenith, RCA, Westinghouse, Motorola, Crosley, Admiral and Magnarox, and came in a variety of cabinet styles with screens ranging from 12 to 20 inches (30-50cm). Television had become the ultimate status symbol. Not to be able to discuss the various programmes was to mark a person as a social outcast. The TV aerial usurped the latest model of car in the driveway as a social badge. *Esquire* commented: 'The next thing they'll be selling is `falsies' - dummy television aerials for owners who are ashamed of not owning a set with its familiar trademark on the roof.'

The television seemed to have become the dominating force of everyday life. In 1951 Van Heusen even brought out a range of TV ties 'with TV-inspired patterns ... designed to keep the gals focused on channel Y-O-U!' But at this time television was still very much an American institution. In 1951 only 6 per cent of British households had a set, and no one would have identified with it to the extent of a TV tie! The Coronation of Queen Elizabeth II in 1953 created a rush to buy sets, and the ceremony was watched by over 20 million viewers, many of whom had not previously watched television.

British television, although showing American films, was, however, completely different from its trans-Atlantic counterpart. Until 1955 there was only one channel, the BBC, and the BBC's charter expressly excluded advertising, while advertising, by means of sponsored shows, financed American TV. Many critics were concerned about the effects of bringing marketing into the living room. As popular interest in psychology grew, awareness of subliminal suggestion increased. Brainwashing or thought control was a common science fiction theme - although in movies such as *Invasion of the Body Snatchers* (1956), the mind-invaders came from outer space rather than General Motors. In any event, the commercial sponsors of TV programmes left the viewers in no doubt as to who brought them the show, although the effect on the viewers gave cause for concern. Despite the much-quoted story from 1950 of the two-year old who could recommend to his mother which brands to buy when supermarket shopping, television and advertising were becoming dependent on each other. By the late fifties Vance Packard could cite a General Foods report that claimed that the average American family was exposed to 117 TV and radio commercials a day, another report that one or more members of a typical family would be exposed to an hour of TV advertising each day, and that, on late-night television, programmes could be seen carrying 15 or more advertisements in a half-hour section. All this echoed earlier complaints of excessive advertising on pre-war radio. One by-product of television advertising was that many

4. Colour television was new to Britain. Here a test for colour is being run. Note the choice selection of sunhats assembled for the occasion.

radio stations, unable to attract sufficient advertising revenue, became 'Black' stations, reaching an audience that generally could not afford to buy television sets. These Black stations contributed towards a desire for self-fulfilment and the development of the civil rights movement, and they also played a large part in the rise in the popularity of rhythm and blues music.

Despite the commercialism, some television, particularly in the early fifties, was of a very high standard, and, paradoxically, this was largely because of the film industry. In an effort to stave off the threat posed by television, film companies would not allow their films (apart from a few dated westerns and children's films) to be shown on the small screen. Television therefore turned to live drama, commissioning plays and adapting novels. It also attracted young actors, and among those who were first seen on TV were Rod Steiger, James Dean, Grace Kelly, Paul Newman and Anne Bancroft. Established Hollywood actors, on the other hand, shunned the new medium - it took $60,000 to persuade Bob Hope to make four 30-minute shows in 1950. Sponsors such as the Philco Television Playhouse, Kraft Television Theatre and the US Steel Hour presented high-quality live drama, with some four hundred plays broadcast in 1951, including *The Great Escape*, George Orwell's *1984* and *Twelve Angry Men*. In the early fifties television was, compared with film, hard work. It went out live, including

4

INTRODUCTION

the commercials, which produced often hilarious fiascos, such as the fridge door that wouldn't close, and the dog that resolutely refused to eat the advertised dog food and walked away in disgust. In addition, the nature of television drama, with its limiting effects of restricted studio space, live editing (with usually only three cameras) and the use of close-ups, did much to influence Hollywood.

THE CINEMA STRIKES BACK

The most obvious way in which the film industry could combat television was in its presentation. As early as the 1920s, attempts had been made to achieve wide-screen projection. Now, with both colour and size obvious advantages in favour of the movie, the film industry looked to new techniques. In 1952, Cinerama was launched. This was a process by which the film was shot on three cameras and then projected, with three projectors, onto a huge wrap-round screen that curved through an arc of 146 degrees, which is about the same as the angle of vision of the human eye. The visual effects of the two-hour long demonstration film *This Is Cinerama* were often spectacular, particularly a realistic roller coaster ride sequence, and stereophonic sound enhanced the experience. For a while Cinerama was all the rage, and there were reports of a Cinerama-burger (the hamburger with the new dimension), a liquor store called Liquorama and even a children's nursery called Kiddirama. Despite this, it never was more than a passing novelty. The expense of the equipment and the size - the screen was 75 feet wide, 26 feet high (23 x 8m) - meant it was suitable only for large cinemas, as the Cinerama souvenir programme admitted: 'It was the ultimate, a luxury entertainment planned for twenty or thirty major cities, for luxury theaters that lent themselves to the demands of its engineering requirements. Cinerama is not meant for local or neighborhood theaters, but as a special event to be enjoyed once or twice a year as new Cinerama productions are available. It is a kind of Metropolitan Opera of the screen.' Obviously the film industry required a more economically practical system.

In 1953 Twentieth Century-Fox introduced CinemaScope, a wide-screen technique that needed only a single projector and a flat screen 68 feet by 24 feet (21 x 7m). *The Robe* (1953) was a biblical epic, notable not only as the first showing of CinemaScope, but also as the Hollywood debut of Richard Burton! Indeed, the epic was to become one of the main weapons in the fight against television (a TV epic would be a contradiction in terms), and although *Quo Vadis?* (1951), the first fifties epic, pre-dates the big-screen experiments, it set the style for a number of large-scale movies, including *Knights of the Round Table* (1953), *Helen of Troy* (1955), *Alexander the Great* (1956), *The Ten Commandments* (1956), *The Vikings* (1958) and *Ben Hur* (1959). As the publicity for *Helen of Troy* declared 'Big

1. Although Richard Nixon was famed as a television communicator, General Eisenhower was the first President to be sold 'like a breakfast food'. While whistle-stop appearances from the Republican campaign train recalled the traditional electioneering style, every move he made was, in fact, planned for the TV cameras.

screens mean big themes!'

An attempt to push film beyond even Cinerama was the brief and zany 3-D craze, which produced some memorable effects and the enduring image of fifties audiences wearing the 3-D glasses that were essential to the system and recoiling in their seats as spears, bullets and lions seemed to spring at them from the screen. The first 3-D movie was *Bwana Devil* (1953), a jungle story that promised 'a lion in your lap'. The process certainly delivered the lion, and briefly 3-D appeared to be the ultimate cinemagraphic form. Warner Brothers' horror movie *House of Wax* (1953), which starred Vincent Price, was the first major film in 3-D - or Natural Vision, as Warner Brothers described it - but although it was successful, the system was dropped as audiences tired of the glasses and of the contrived effects other films introduced to exploit the process. CinemaScope, the best system to date, belonged to Twentieth Century-Fox. Paramount countered with VistaVision, and meanwhile Mike Todd developed Todd-AO, which used wide film stock to create the big look of *Oklahoma* (1955) and *Around the World in Eighty Days* (1956).

44

2

3

Further technical developments included an improved CinemaScope (CinemaScope 55) and Technirama, but by then television and cinema had begun to work together. As well as being an avid consumer of old movies, television sometimes acted as the testing ground for new ideas; *Marty*, for instance, a television play about ordinary people, was made into a highly successful film in 1956. The closest collaboration between film and TV was achieved by the Walt Disney Company, which ran a TV series called *Disneyland* that advertised the theme park Disneyland, which had been opened in 1954, as well as showing Disney feature films and shorts. Disney also made programmes for television - a three-part serial about Davy Crockett, which captured the imagination of the nation's small boys whose demands for a coonskin hat made furriers rich and the household cat fear for its life, was subsequently joined together and released as a feature-length movie.

TELEVISION ENTERS POLITICS

While all this was going on, television was revealing another, powerful side. As early as 1948 the seeds of what was to become an important association of TV and politics had been laid. In 1948, acting on the advice of the Republicans' advertising agency, John Dewey had played to the cameras. Dewey lost to Harry S. Truman (who had avoided television), but the pattern had been established. From then on television was a crucial factor in all campaigns. By 1952, when there were estimated to be 15 million sets in the US, the Eisenhower/Stevenson campaign was directed at the TV audience, which at the same time was being targeted by Westinghouse, who sponsored NBC to the tune of $3.5 million. Not only did Americans watch images of

2. Nicknamed 'the killer', Jerry Lee Lewis was one of the all-time wild men of rock-and-roll. On one occasion, piqued because Chuck Berry was chosen to close a show, he set light to his piano, with the comment, 'I'd like to see the S.O.B. try to follow that'.

3. Although the cinema took to rock-and-roll - 'Rock Around the Clock' was used behind the credits of The Blackboard Jungle *- and allegedly contributed to the popularisation of the sound, television, hamstrung by sponsors, was more reluctant. When Elvis Presley finally appeared on* The Ed Sullivan Show, *he was shown from the waist up lest his pelvic gyrations cause offence.*

Eisenhower and Stevenson, there was Betty Furness opening and closing fridge doors throughout the campaign, which included $1.5 million worth of scripted spots, during which Eisenhower pretended to answer questions from Joe Public. Stevenson, who refused to do spots 'like a breakfast food', lost. Eisenhower's running mate, Richard Nixon, made history by appearing on nationwide television to repudiate charges of corruption in the famous Checkers speech. Such were the levels of commercialisation that TV advertisers wanted to sponsor the speech, which was expected to be watched in every home. In the event, sponsors were turned down so as not to detract from the importance of the occasion.

Public opinion, through television, made Nixon, just as, two years later, it destroyed Senator McCarthy, whose true nature was revealed in the televised hearings during which Joseph Welch's reproach 'You have done enough. Have you no sense of decency?' still echoes down the years as one of the great moments of televised history.

The standards of decency and integrity of television were again called into question, and the end of the decade saw the collapse of one of the mainstays of fifties TV, the quiz show. By 1955 television was such an essential advertising medium that sponsoring a successful show was an integral part of marketing. Revlon, the cosmetics firm, introduced a new generation of quiz games, which had hitherto been small affairs, with *The $64,000 Question*, 'the biggest jackpot in history', when even the loser got a Cadillac as a consolation prize. Other quiz games soon appeared - *The $64,000 Challenge, High Finance, Twenty-One* and *Giant Step* all vied for high ratings by offering larger and larger prizes. *Twenty-One* became one of the most popular, and contestant Charles Van Doren, a university English teacher with clean-cut looks and an earnest, serious manner, became a cult figure as, week after week, he plumbed his memory for elusive answers. At one stage his winnings were up to $130,000. Unfortunately, in 1958 it was revealed that the show was fixed, and the production team of *The $64,000 Question* and *The $64,000 Challenge* testified to the House of Representatives that Revlon had dictated which contestant should be allowed forward to the big prize and which should be dropped.

Television, which had started the fifties as an under-financed David taking on the Hollywood Goliath, ended the decade under a cloud of commercialism and corruption.

INFLUENCES

1. Much television and radio comedy can be seen as directly descending from the vaudeville acts in which many of the stars had developed. Comedian Arthur Askey was a popular figure.

2. The Babylon set from Intolerance (1916) conveys something of the massive scale of the early film spectacles. The need to combat the challenge posed by television with big-screen presentation led to the revival of the epic, usually with a biblical theme, as a cinematic art form.

3. The Grapes of Wrath (1940) was a forerunner of the social documentary movie, whose realism and message contrasted with the 'entertainment' motive that had become the cinema's main function.

4. The influence of sponsorship on US television was so great that the main criterion of a show's value was the ratings - the number of viewers who tuned in to watch it and, of course, the sponsor's advertising. This brought a new term into our language- 'soap opera' - to describe the continuing stories, pioneered on radio by Palmolive in the twenties, which soap manufacturers thought would give them a predominantly female audience.

5. The 'Jump' rhythm and blues of Big Joe Turner provided one of the musical strands that was to be fused into the new sound of rock-and-roll, although when Bill Haley came to record Turner's hit 'Shake, Rattle and Roll', the lyrics, originally written for a worldly-wise black audience, suffered the fate of many such songs in being sanitised for the white teenage market.

BIG SCREENS, BIG THEMES

1

2

1. 'Big screens mean big themes' was the motto of the cinema now enhanced by new projection techniques, and although by 1959, when Ben Hur was made, the novelty was over, a powerful story combined with a running time of three and a half hours of breathtaking spectacle (which complemented, rather than overshadowed the theme) resulted in the ultimate epic. Costing $15 million to produce and the winner of 11 Academy Awards, it is still one of the most successful films ever made.

2. The chariot race had been one of the great scenes of the 1926 version, and director William Wyler, who had worked on that production was aware that modern audiences would demand a spectacular treatment. Coordinated by the legendary stuntman Yakima Canutt, it is regarded by many film historians as the definitive action sequence.

3

4

5

3. The Ten Commandments (1956) combined the technology of fifties cinema with the essentially pre-war dream world of old Hollywood. This was perhaps inevitable as it was both produced and directed by Cecil B. de Mille in an attempt to update his 1923 silent movie treatment of the same story. His dated, often over-the-top approach did not detract from the film's commercial success, and with its often spectacular scenes and, literally, cast of thousands (including Charlton Heston as Moses), it exists as an anachronistic example of the commercial epic.

4. Quo Vadis? (1951) was the first of the decade's ancient history epics. Designed initially to woo audiences away from their televisions and back to the cinema, the epic became a uniquely cinematographic experience.

5. King Vidor's War and Peace (1956) was an exception to the main run of fifties epics in not being set in biblical times. Despite this, in all other respects, including the mandatory spectacular set pieces and the 'big' theme, it was very much in the epic mould.

THE FILM MAKERS

1

2

1. The Seventh Seal, 1957, established Bergman as a major film maker. Both his direction and the camera-work of Gunnar Fischer transformed the story, an allegory of life and death, good and evil, set at the time of the Black Death, into a series of visually stunning encounters. The black and white treatment was itself almost the hallmark of 'art' cinema at a time when colour was regarded as a prerequisite of commercial films.

2. François Truffaut's Les Quatre Cents Coups (The Four Hundred Blows, 1958), the first of a semi-autobiographical quartet of films in which Jean-Pierre Léaud played the same character progressing from child to adulthood, created a sensation as the first example of nouvelle vague, a form of cinéma verité which avoided contrivance to the point where there were no apparent signs of direction or editing.

4

3

5

3. *Akira Kurosawa's* Rashomon *(1950) received universal acclaim at the Venice Film Festival in 1951. At a time when interest in Japanese art and design generally was growing, the film revealed to the West the hitherto unknown art of Japanese cinema. Like* The Seventh Seal, *it is set in the Middle Ages, and its story, too, is allegorical and mystical. Kurosawa's lighting and camera technique, as well as the treatment of the themes of rape and murder and the cult of the samurai, seemed uniquely Japanese, yet such was the cross-fertilisation of cultures that his 1954 film* Seven Samurai *was a self-declared tribute to the westerns of John Ford and was itself the inspiration for the 1960 movie,* The Magnificent Seven.

4. Le Notte di Cabiria *(Nights of Cabiria, 1957) represents the last work of Federico Fellini in the small film genre. Continuing the low-life theme of* La Strada, Le Notte di Cabiria *too starred Giulietta Masina, this time as a prostitute, who represents total innocence.*

5. *Fellini's* La Strada *(The Road, 1954) is, even now, a memorable example of Italian cinema, its poignant story echoed in its haunting theme music. The film relates the tragi-comical lives of the itinerant strongman Zampano (Antony Quinn in his first major role), the childlike Gelsomina (Fellini's gamine-like wife Giulietta Masina) and Matto, the fool (Richard Basehart).*

REACH FOR THE STARS

1. Guys and Dolls (1955) is mainly memorable for the teaming of Frank Sinatra with Marlon Brando, who, after the success of The Wild One and On the Waterfront (both 1954), was seeking to distance himself from the image in which he felt he might be typecast. As was typical of film musicals, Guys and Dolls had originated as a stage show (1950), with songs by Frank Loesser in a musical comedy adaptation of Damon Runyon's stories.

2. On the Town, starring Frank Sinatra and Gene Kelly and directed by Gene Kelly and Stanley Donen, gave the film musical a new direction by linking the song and dance element more closely with the overall story than had previously been thought necessary. Filming much of the action on the streets of New York rather than in the studio gave it an additional dimension.

3. Sam Goldwyn's final film was Porgy and Bess (1959). Gershwin's famous musical became a glorious cinematic tour de force under the direction of Otto Preminger. Ken Darby and André Previn won Oscars for their musical direction of songs such as 'Summertime'.

1

4. The Rodgers and Hammerstein musical Oklahoma was already a successful stage show when, like other stage musicals - South Pacific, Pal Joey, The King and I, Carmen Jones and Guys and Dolls, for example - it was made into a film in 1955. Produced by Fred Zinnemann, its panoramic landscape proved an ideal vehicle for Mike Todd's new wide-screen technique, Todd-AO.

5. The King and I was another Rodgers and Hammerstein stage musical that was transferred to the screen. The film version (1956) starred Yul Brynner, who had found fame in the original Broadway production.

THE ANTI-HERO

1

2

3

1. Tony Curtis, whose early career had suggested that he was destined for nothing but teenage heart-throb roles, had successfully paired with Burt Lancaster in Trapeze (1956). A year later, in Sweet Smell of Success, he again played opposite Lancaster. Curtis was cast as an ambitious, manipulative 'gofer' (press agent), while Lancaster was a corrupt, power-mad newspaper columnist. It was filmed in black and white entirely on location in New York.

2. The Caine Mutiny (1954) had already provoked controversy as a novel before being filmed with Humphrey Bogart as the tragically vulnerable, paranoid Captain Queeg. Ill with cancer, this was a different Bogart from the laconic tough-guys of the forties or even the reprobate Charlie Allnutt in The African Queen (1951). Suddenly, he seemed smaller, his own physical ill-health mirrored in the mental sickness of the character.

3. Loosely based on a real event that took place in 1947, The Wild One (1954), with its portrayal of a nomadic gang of motorcyclists, became the first youth cult movie. Marlon Brando as the gang-leader, Johnny, was the archetypal anti-hero. Mean and tough-looking in black leather, Brando spoke the words that became the nihilistic theme of the delinquent. Asked, 'What are you rebelling against?', Brando replies: 'What've you got?'

4. Rebel without a Cause (1955) was, like The Wild One, a teenage movie elevated by the quality of its main actor, this time James Dean. But while Brando maintained that he was simply bringing his actor's craft to his role, Dean was seen to identify and empathise with the character Jim, who, although coming from an affluent background, is consumed with the anger and frustration that were the themes of disaffected youth throughout the fifties.

5. The British cult of angry young men took its lead from John Osborne's play Look Back In Anger (1956), which critic Kenneth Tynan saw as presenting 'post-war youth as it really is'. With Richard Burton taking the part of Jimmy Porter, it was made into a film in 1959, and although successfully capturing the essence of the play, it had, in the intervening years, lost some of its ability to shock that the play had had.

6. Taken from John Braine's novel, the film Room at the Top (1959) was seen as an example of cinéma verité. 'It states what a northern town is like: cobbled streets, smudged views of chimneys, women cooking at ranges, wet slabs of washing to be dodged by children playing in the streets,' commented critic Penelope Gilliatt. But more than the landscape, it portrayed a class-ridden society, of which the 'top' could be reached only through corruption and sexual manipulation. Laurence Harvey portrayed Joe Lampton, the suave but ruthless anti-hero.

MOVIE QUEENS

1. In Billy Wilder's 1955 comedy The Seven Year Itch, *Marilyn Monroe* portrayed the ultimate sexual ingénue, *innocently tormenting her downstairs neighbour, played by Tom Ewell, with a stream of provocative images. In the heat of a New York summer, she keeps her panties in the ice box and sleeps in the nude. In one of cinema's most famous scenes, Monroe's skirts blow revealingly when she stands over a subway grating as she parodies her own image.*

2. After the success of Wilder's Some Like It Hot, Let's Make Love, *Monroe's penultimate film, was a sad anti-climax. Directed by George Cukor, with whom Monroe worked again on* Something's Got to Give, *and co-starring Yves Montand, the movie neither did justice to the 'old' Marilyn nor provided the new direction that she sought in* The Misfits *and* Something's Got to Give.

3. The British actress Diana Dors, *seen here in* The Unholy Wife (1957), *joined the parade of bosomy blondes, which included Marilyn Monroe, Marie Wilson, Jayne Mansfield, and Mamie Van Doren.*

4

All the sultry drama of Tennessee Williams' Pulitzer Prize Play is now on the screen!

M·G·M presents

Cat on a Hot Tin Roof

This is Maggie the Cat...

starring ELIZABETH TAYLOR
PAUL NEWMAN
BURL IVES

JACK CARSON · JUDITH ANDERSON

Screen Play by RICHARD BROOKS and JAMES POE · Based on the Play "CAT ON A HOT TIN ROOF" by TENNESSEE WILLIAMS
in METROCOLOR · AN AVON PRODUCTION · Directed by RICHARD BROOKS · Produced by LAWRENCE WEINGARTEN

5

6

4. Grace Kelly turned her back on the movies when she married Prince Rainier of Monaco in 1956. Her last film, To Catch a Thief (1955), co-starring Cary Grant, seemed to merge present fantasy with future reality in its rich Riviera setting.

5. Like Gina Lollobrigida, Sophia Loren's acting abilities transcended her initial cheesecake image, although her first major English-language picture, The Pride And The Passion (1957), served more to show off her body than her talent.

6. The films Elizabeth Taylor made in the fifties - Giant (1956) Raintree County (1958), Cat on a Hot Tin Roof (1958) and Suddenly Last Summer (1959) - allowed her screen persona to, albeit temporarily, eclipse her Hollywood image. Playing opposite Paul Newman in Tennessee Williams' Cat on a Hot Tin Roof, she was sensuous, vulnerable and violent.

7

7. Baby Doll (1956), written by Tennessee Williams, was, according to Time 'possibly the dirtiest American picture ever legally exhibited', and that sort of condemnation naturally made it a box office success. The controversy was caused by the film's refusal to romanticise the unattractive nature of its characters and by the sexuality of Carroll's Baker's 'baby doll'.

HIHO, SILVER

1. High Noon (1952) ranks not just as a great western but as a great movie. It differed from traditional westerns with their panoramic scenery and big, set-piece action scenes. The innovative portrayal of western townspeople as self-interested and cowardly rather than as heroic characters was such a cultural shock that it was seen as contributing to writer Carl Foreman's being black-listed as a communist.

2. Successful westerns were built on strong storylines, and The Tall Men (1955), directed by Raoul Walsh, contained two classic plot elements - a journey (in this case a cattle drive from Texas to Montana) and two men competing for the possession of a woman (Clark Gable and Robert Ryan for Jane Russell).

3. Having started as a radio series, The Lone Ranger first appeared on television in 1949, and with an heroic theme tune from the 'William Tell' overture and the cry 'Hi Ho Silver!', the masked man (Clayton Moore), his faithful Indian companion Tonto (Jay Silverheels) and his horse Silver became part of our popular heritage. In many ways a sort of Batman and Robin on the hoof, the stories, simplistic in plot and characterisation, always ensured that good triumphed over evil, while the Lone Ranger's little homilies that rounded off the programmes ensured that, on the small screen at least, the western stood for the best of the American way of life.

4. *Ward Bond in Wagon Train (1957). The success of Cheyenne in 1955 opened the door to a flood of TV westerns. They were particularly favoured by the TV companies because of their low production costs - stock footage of unmemorable scenes or leftovers from big-screen productions could easily be incorporated to give a big effect from a small budget. Although these western soap operas proved to be the springboard for actors such as Clint Eastwood (Rawhide), Dennis Weaver (Gunsmoke) and James Garner (Maverick), they relied in the main on unknowns to keep costs down.*

4

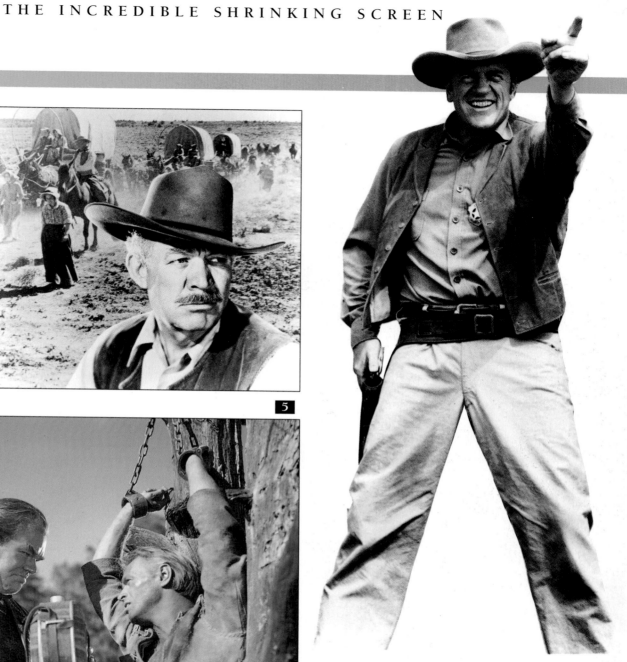

5

6

5. The Last Wagon (1956), directed by Delmer Daves, starred Richard Widmark. Its themes were favourites with western directors - a man survives tragedy (the murder of his Indian wife and children), takes revenge on the murderers and suffers physical hardship leading a wagon train before starting a new life in a new place.

6. James Arness as Marshal Matt Dillon starred in the popular TV western Gunsmoke. By 1958, 30 different western series filled prime-time television, with Gunsmoke from CBS topping the ratings at 30.8 per cent. So popular was the series that even at the end of the sixties it was still in the top ten.

REPORTING THE NEWS

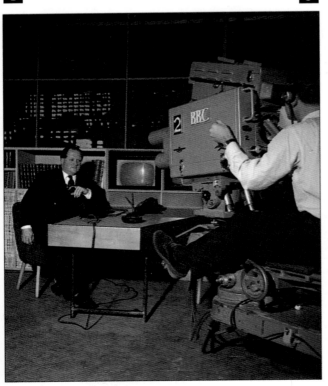

1. The 1954 McCarthy hearings before a Senate committee were the first government processes to have been televised, reaching an audience estimated at up to 20 million. Under the glare of television lights, the Senator, whose witch hunt for communists in government office had made him a feared and powerful figure, seemed to shrink. The spell was broken, and Eisenhower could joke that 'McCarthyism is now McCarthywasm'.

2. The Eisenhower/Stevenson presidential election of 1952, learning from the televised campaign of 1948, was conducted with TV audiences in mind. From then on, no politician could afford to ignore television. This picture shows President Eisenhower's inauguration parade (1953).

3. Richard Dimbleby, a pioneer television journalist, is shown presenting the BBC's current affairs programme Panorama in 1956.

4. Ed Sullivan was one of the most enduring of all television personalities. His first show, Toast of the Town (later The Ed Sullivan Show), began in 1948 and soon headed the ratings, attracting the sponsorship of the Ford Motor Company

5, 6, 7 & 8. The coronation of Queen Elizabeth (1953) was the first major event to receive international television exposure. NBC devised a system by which the BBC's coverage was filmed off a television in London and immediately developed in a portable processor. A special plane, equipped as an airborne editing studio, flew to Boston where the film, by then edited, was broadcast. In the States, viewing was interrupted by advertisements, many of which were given a royal theme to capitalise on the occasion. This was cited by those opposed to the idea of commercial television for Britain (which at the time had only one channel - the BBC) as an example of the perils of allowing advertising on TV.

1

2

3

1. Although at the time of this picture - 1957 - colour television was not available to British audiences, the glamour, even in black and white, of Victor Sylvester's Dancing Club put the BBC show in the top six ratings.

2. The absence of commercial sponsorship, or even prizes, meant that, unlike their American counterparts, British quiz shows were sedate, innocuous parlour games. Here, presenter Eamonn Andrews hosts the popular BBC quiz What's my line in 1952.

3. Airtime for recorded music was restricted, and many hits were more often heard through the interpretation of BBC musicians than in the original version. A popular exception was Family Favourites, a long-running radio show, whose dedications made it particularly favoured as a link with British servicemen posted abroad. In this 1955 picture, the programme's presenter, Jean Metcalfe, is seen with entertainer Max Bygraves.

1

1. Lucille Ball, starring with her husband Desi Arnaz in the long-running I Love Lucy show, was America's favourite television comedienne. The show's zany spoofs of suburban domestic life shot it to the top of the ratings within six months of its first showing in 1952, and within its first year Ball and Arnaz made TV history with a contract worth $8 million. At the peak of its popularity, the show attracted 50 million viewers.

2. Phil Silvers as the scheming Sergeant Ernie Bilko, was another television favourite, especially as war-time memories or the draft itself made military life relevant to most of the audience. Although many of the fifties references are lost, the shows are still popular when re-shown.

3. British television also drew on music hall and radio for its first generation of entertainers, and this traditional comedy form remained popular in spite of the competition offered by television. It was only when a truly British style of comedy evolved with the emergence of Tony Hancock from radio, that UK television stopped depending on American imports or incorporating what were virtually music-hall acts into general entertainment programmes.

4. The comedy team of George Burns and Gracie Allen was already popular on radio in the thirties, alongside Fred Allen, Jack Benny and the Marx Brothers, all of whom eventually moved into television. CBS regarded the securing of Benny, Burns and Allen in the early days of television as a major step in attracting mass audiences.

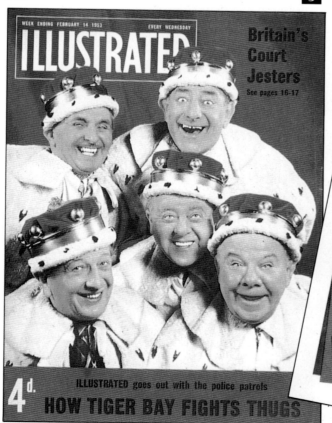

ROCK-AND-ROLL

1

2

1. Elvis Presley, 'the King', can be credited with popularising the fusion of southern music - black, rhythm and blues, country music and even church music - into the sound that was rock-and-roll, fulfilling the dream for a white singer with 'the negro sound and negro feel'. His looks, dress and stage act brought him notoriety as the first rock star, a symbol of the teenage emancipation that dominated the decade.

2. Buddy Holly, with what has been described as 'that almost meek Clark Kent façade with the glasses, tie and suit', appeared to be the antithesis of Elvis. His death in a plane crash together with the Big Bopper and Richie Valens on 'the day that music died' put him alongside James Dean as a cult figure whose posthumous fame and influence continues.

3. History may find it strange that the kiss-curled, middle-aged-looking Bill Haley should be at the centre of the first rock-and-roll riots, but it was the use of his song 'Rock Around the Clock' in the 1955 film The Blackboard Jungle rather than the man himself that linked rock with rebellion.

4. Although Cliff Richard's background lacked the complex influences that gave the original rock-and-rollers their vitality, he nevertheless produced some acceptable pastiches of rock-and-roll before settling down into a still-continuing career as a popular singer.

5. Rock-and-roll became synonymous with teenage violence, and its condemnation by parents, teachers, church and youth leaders and the press only fuelled the flames. The caption to this 1957 picture from Milan, Italy, notes that the police had to intervene to control 'hundreds of rock-and-roll crazed teenagers', who were unable to gain admittance to a dance.

Frank Lloyd Wright, civic centre, 1957.

CHAPTER THREE

GLASSHOUSES

'THE THINGS WE LIVE WITH, THE THINGS WE FASHION FOR OURSELVES TO MAKE OUR WORK, OUR LEISURE, OUR HOMES AND OUR PUBLIC PLACES CONFORM TO OUR STANDARDS OF WHAT IS RIGHT AND ACCEPTABLE WILL INEVITABLY FORM A PATTERN FOR FUTURE HISTORIANS AS TO WHAT WE STOOD FOR...'

PETER MULLER-MUNK, 1955

INTRODUCTION

Architecture in many ways symbolises the visual aura of the age, with strongly identifiable images masking a mass of contradictions. Gordon Bunshaft's Lever House, New York (1952) - 'the mother of all the glass boxes,' as Tom Wolfe described it - or Ludwig Mies van der Rohe and Philip Johnson's the Seagram Building, also New York (1956-8) can be seen as 'typically' fifties, and the image of these buildings and buildings like them appeared in cities across the world throughout the decade and into the sixties. Yet just as typical of the age are Eero Saarinen's sweeping curves of the Yale University hockey rink and the TWA Terminal at Kennedy Airport, New York, or Jørn Utzon's Sydney Opera House (1957), while in another mode, the commercial 'populuxe' of Morris Lapidus's kitsch hotels, Miami's Eden Roc and Fontainebleau, might claim to represent the decade, even though to a purist to mention Eden Roc on the same page as the Seagram Building is a heresy.

Alongside these existed the disciples, the 'wannabes' and the plagiarists, some go-it-alone individualists as well as the great mass of quasi-architects who built the sprawling suburbs with their picture-windowed, colonial-fronted, ranch-style-plus-car-port, modern homes, and the shopping malls and bowling alleys and drive-in eateries that also symbolise the period.

THE BAUHAUS INFLUENCE

Above all, however, there is the unique contradiction that, against the general trend towards Americanism that was apparent in a whole range of consumer goods, the roots of major American city architecture lay in Europe. The reason for this is simple. Unlike rock-and-roll, car styles or advertising jingles, architecture is a long-term business. Fads and isms occur, but they cannot be treated in the same flamboyant way in which General Motors could give cars chrome breasts or fins and then discard them overnight in favour of something else. Planned obsolescence is not a feature of architecture, and the architect regards him- or herself as a former, not a follower, of public taste. The major influence in this century on intellectual and philosophical, as well as on practical design aesthetics, was the Bauhaus, which had always promoted what came to be called Internationalism, so that cultural heritage and folk traditions, the eccentricity of individualism, decoration and decadence were all subordinated to 'pure' design.

Walter Gropius, the founder-director of the Bauhaus, left Germany in 1928 and moved to England in 1934 where he practised as an architect. In 1937 he accepted a senior teaching post at Harvard and was appointed Dean of Architecture the following year. As the rise of Naziism made the continuance of the Bauhaus impossible, other leading figures, as well as many students, left. In 1937 Mies van der Rohe, who had headed the Bauhaus in its final years, went

1

2

1. Although built in the manner of Le Corbusier, the United Nations Headquarters, New York (1947-50), is of historical interest rather for the circumstances under which it was built than for its style. The site was donated by John D. Rockefeller, and the design was by an international committee of architects including Le Corbusier himself, with the American Wallace Kirkman Harrison (who later supervised the design of the Lincoln Center) as principal architect.

2. Farnsworth House (1950) by Mies van der Rohe is characterised by its 'floating slabs' of terrace, floor and roof supported by a metal structure. Although its glass walls give it a superficial similarity to Philip Johnson's Glass House, it is far more a prototype for the Crown Hall at Chicago's Illinois Institute of Technology.

to the USA, becoming Dean of Architecture at the Illinois Institute of Technology the next year, and, quite literally, the architect of that newly formed Institute, designing 21 buildings for the campus.

In 1937, Norma K. Stahse of the Association of Arts and Industries in Chicago invited Walter Gropius to form a new Bauhaus in Chicago. Precluded from doing so by his responsibilities at Harvard, Gropius recommended that the post be offered to László Moholy-Nagy, who had fled from Germany in 1937. After a false start through lack of funds, the new Bauhaus got under way in 1939, with Moholy-Nagy as director and Gropius as consultant. In 1944 it became known as the Institute of Design, finally, in 1949, becoming integrated with the Illinois Institute of Technology. But to suggest, as Tom Wolfe has done, that these were 'uprooted, exhausted, penniless men without a country, battered by fate' is not only untrue but also misinterprets the true background. American major architecture had, by the mid-1930s, reached a stalemate.

THE ACCEPTANCE OF INTERNATIONALISM

The great symbol, the skyscraper, had become uneconomic to build; as Henry McBride had pointed out: 'When it pays to spend $56 million building an Empire State Building, skyscrapers will continue to be built. When millions are lost in their construction, they will no longer be constructed.' Furthermore, the decorative elements of skyscraper architecture had already become dated. It was the needs of the future that prompted the institutions of learning to look

to those who had been responsible not only for establishing the dominant aesthetics of modern architecture but also for researching into materials and construction techniques.

This endorsement of Internationalism set the scene for much of the fifties. The public became aware of this in the late forties. Philip Johnson, a disciple of Mies van der Rohe and former director of the architectural department of the Museum of Modern Art (when he had coined the term International Style), built the Glass House at New Canaan, Connecticut (1949-50). Actually, this was two single-storey structures: the main house, 32 by 56 feet (9.7 x 17m) was completely walled in clear glass. The interior was entirely open plan, with only the bathroom area screened. One hundred feet away, a contrasting structure almost without windows housed guest quarters, a gallery and study. *Life* featured it, reporting that Johnson considered it a success. Unfortunately, his mentor, Mies van der Rohe, fared less well with his glass house, the Farnsworth House near Plano, Illinois, which was completed in 1951. His client declared the place uninhabitable and started legal action.

Flat-roofed buildings, with areas of open-plan living and large windows, already existed - Frank Lloyd Wright's pre-war Usonian houses, which had included a 1938 commission from *Life* to design 'a modern home' - but it was Johnson's Glass House that directly introduced the large glass area and open-plan living space, although these were rationalised into picture windows and a quasi-open plan style. Both these features had the advantage of instantly identifying a house as 'modern'. Other signs were a flat roof, which then made it 'Californian Modern', particularly if it had an overhang, and a car porch. And while big glass boxes, usually sorry parodies of the Miesian concept, started to appear everywhere as offices and institutions, smaller boxes sprang up as housing, and so the landscape changed.

Now that 'modern' could disguise cheap construction, the expansion of the consumer boom of the fifties could be accommodated equally quickly. Generally, there was an exodus from city centres, as new industry, particularly those based on electronics and plastics, provided employment away from traditional industrial areas. Soon the new suburbs - often referred to as Levittowns after William J. Levitt, a major builder of economy housing - ate into the farmlands and sometimes converged, so that the link between, for example, Fort Worth and Dallas, or between the small towns and suburbs round Los Angeles, began to create mega-cities. It is surely ironic that the Bauhaus, whose ideals had originally encompassed the need to design socialist housing for the masses, should, however indirectly, have contributed so much to the ultimate consumer society.

The link between consumerism and mass housing was absolute. Not only did it open up the potential of lifestyle marketing, but it created the need for a whole range of other buildings. Churches of all denominations became important

1. Mies van der Rohe's buildings for the Illinois Institute of Technology (1946-56) demonstrated the pure formalism that characterised his work. Crown Hall, housing the School of Architecture (1956), features a floor area that appears to float above ground level.

1

as focal points for new communities, each church asserting its individuality in its design style. Supermarkets, which had started to appear outside towns in the forties, shook off their warehouse look and became vast, brightly lit, meccas of commerce set in an acre of tarmac to accommodate car-orientated shopping. The effect of the car was seen everywhere, though the 1958 concept of the open-plan home incorporating the garage, which had been promoted by *House and Garden,* never caught on. The fifties love of the car never went quite that far. It did, however, exemplify how far the traditional concept of the home, with its compartmentalised areas, had been eroded.

REBUILDING BRITAIN - NEW BRUTALISM
In Britain architects faced different problems from those facing their colleagues in America. As with the rest of Europe, bombs had left indiscriminate holes in the cities, and the priority was to rebuild houses and industry. The opportunity to offer better housing was grasped in the building of New Towns, such as Stevenage, Harlow, Basildon and Crawley. Despite the opportunity to adopt the technology (if not the social ideology) of the Bauhaus, as the Americans had done, the established Modern movement in Britain favoured a style known as the New Humanism, a Scandinavian-derived form of Modernism that emphasised the 'warm' qualities of wood-framed windows, brickwork and tiled roofs. This sort of foot-in-both-camps attitude, which can be seen in British post-war design in general, was challenged by the school of New Brutalism. The name, synonymous with the two young architects, Peter and Alison Smithson, was seen as a defiant rebuttal of the New Humanism. The first New Brutalist building was the Secondary School at Hunstanton (1949-54). Here the Smithsons not only avoided any romantic decorative features, but exaggerated the functionalism of the design by leaving exposed plumbing and electric conduiting.

Brutalism succeeded in ousting New Humanism, although the major challenge to the old order, particularly for public buildings such as schools, came from the need for cost-effective construction, especially pre-fabrication. Pre-fabricated structures were first used extensively in the single-storey 'pre fabs', introduced as temporary housing for those made homeless from the Blitz. In common with the rest of the world, the curtain wall, glass box structure, in the manner of the Seagram Building, became the standard form for most commercial buildings.

THE INTERNATIONAL STYLE IN EUROPE
At the same time, the International Style influenced worker-housing projects. In France Le Corbusier designed several such projects, the first of which was the Unité d'Habitation in Marseilles (1946-52). Based on the principles of *La Ville Radieuse,* Unité d'Habitation was commissioned by the government as a prototype for low-cost housing and contained 337 apartments. Le Corbusier had been interested in multiple living units since the 1920s (including his designs in 1922 for a city of 3 million inhabitants). His disciple, Minoru Yamasaki, architect of the World Trade Center, New York (1962-77), was less successful with the Pruitt-Igoe housing estate in St Louis (1952-5). Although the project received an award from the American Institute of Architects, it was, in social terms, a failure and was demolished in 1972. In England, the local government authorities commissioned similar large-scale housing estates, the most famous being the Le Corbusier-inspired Roehampton Estate (1953-6), designed to provide homes for 10,000 people.

With the advantage of hindsight we can see the inherent problems of much of the public housing. Whether they were the result of cynical political motivation (as with Britain's Herbert Morrison), of a misinterpretation of Le Corbusier, or of social factors, which not only occurred with high-density projects but, in another form, with the alleged consumer based-identity neurosis of the US suburbs (as described in Spectorsky's *The Exurbanities),* it is likely that the excesses of public housing will be the least enduring of fifties architecture.

2

THE FESTIVAL OF BRITAIN

More in line with the general euphoria of the fifties were the individualist buildings and projects. In Britain the post-war climate of the Welfare State, which was responsible for the major education and housing projects, had a transitory injection of frivolity with the Festival of Britain in 1951. Designed as a morale-boosting 'tonic to the nation', the Festival was, in fact, a confused mixture of space-age and Victorianism, high-tech and kitsch. Some, like science-fiction writer Brian Aldiss, saw the Dome of Discovery, which was designed by Ralf Tubbs and which was, at the time, the biggest dome ever built, and Powell and Moya's needle-thin obelisk, the Skylon, as symbolising a futuristic Britain. Others, cynically, claimed the symbolism was that, like the country, they had little visible means of support! Of the entire exhibition, only the Royal Festival Hall, designed by Robert Matthew, Sir J.L. Martin, Peter Moro and Edwin Williams, was intended as a permanent structure, and it is now generally accepted that many of the architectural features, particularly the use of colour panels, although suitable for a temporary exhibition, had a debasing effect when incorporated as a decorative feature in mock-International Style architecture. Sir Misha Black, one of the festival's architects, accused it of releasing 'a flood of the worst kind of bastardised modern architecture'.

It should, however, be remembered that during the fifties Britain was suffering from a confusion of cultural and aesthetic identities, and these, together with planning restrictions that limited the height of buildings to 100 feet (30m), or about ten storeys, would in any event have inhibited the assertive architecture that was being attempted in the United States. The two major moves into the future owed nothing to science-fiction styling, but rather to solid technological achievement. Britain, with a major aircraft industry, had pioneered jet travel. London Airport designed by Sir Frederick Gibberd (1955), although understated when compared with St Louis Airport (George Hellmath, Joseph Weinweber and Minoru Yamasaki, 1953-5) or with Idlewild (later Kennedy) Airport, was designed to meet the new needs of air travel. In the United States, where competition for prestige rather than any great love of art was the main motivation for commerce commissioning major architecture, the 'Flying Saucer' Pan Am Building and the even more spectacular TWA Terminal, by Eero Saarinen, were produced. Air travel was so crucial to the development of a fifties aesthetic, that it was really more the Jet Age than the Space Age. Above all, however, it was the Atomic Age. Gibberd designed the first Atomic Power Station at Hinkley Point in 1956. A year later, the World's Fair in Brussels had as its symbol the Atomium, 'Dedicated to the peaceful use of Atomic Energy'.

2. Son of the architect Eliel Eero Saarinen took over from his father the General Motors Technical Institute, Warren, Michigan, as his first important commission (1946-55) a building which shows the influence of Mies van der Rohe. Eero Saarinen's subsequent work includes the Krege Auditorium and the chapel at MIT, the Ingalls hockey rink at Yale, Dulles Airport and the TWA building at Idlewild (Kennedy Airport), New York (seen here), all of which exhibit the fluid, suspended roof structures for which he is best known.

INFLUENCES

1. *The De la Warr pavilion at Bexhill, Sussex, Britain, was designed in 1935 by Serge Chermayeff (b.1900). Chermayeff, who became President and Director of the Institute of Design in Chicago in 1946, here demonstrated the Baubaus criterion of structure devoid of extraneous decoration, which characterised post-Baubaus architecture.*

2. *Le Corbusier, whose Swiss Hostel for the Cité Universitaire, Paris, (1931-2) is shown here, had a profound influence on post-war architecture. However much of what followed, such as the Roehampton Housing Estate, tended to be little more than a superficial copy of his style.*

3. *The Kaufmann Desert House, Palm Springs, (1946) by Richard Neutra (b.1892) represents an early example of Bauhaus-inspired architecture, which became known in the United States as International style.*

4. The Bauhaus buildings at Dessau (1925), designed by Walter Gropius, housed the school until it moved to Berlin in 1928. Although the buildings themselves are a development from an early work, the Fagus Factory of 1911-14, they represent, in conjunction with the work that was carried out within them, the roots of mainstream post-war architecture.

5. The organic structures of Antoni Gaudi (1852-1926), typified in this detail of the Casa Mil· flats, Barcelona (1905-7), resulted from his interest in structural engineering, which he saw as exemplified in the great medieval buildings. Gaudi revitalised a kind of architecture that celebrated pure engineering for its own sake and made possible much of the work of Le Corbusier and the parabolic structures of Nervi and Saarinen.

6. Frank Lloyd Wright (1867-1959) has been credited with giving American architecture the confidence and vision to make it the dominant force in the International style. Although his work during the Twenties and early Thirties was seen as too romantic, Falling Water house at Bear Run, Pennsylvania (1936-7) is regarded as a turning point, embracing as it does much of the European philosophy that formed the basis of the International Modern style.

REBUILDING EUROPE

1. *This 1951 scene of a family viewing housing in the new satellite town of Crawley, Sussex, England, was being repeated all over the world as the massive post-war rebuilding programme got under way.*

2. *Le Corbusier's Unité d'Habitation, built at Marseilles between 1946 and 1952, is an example of the Brutalist style of architecture, the structural concrete is left to show the texture of the rough wood forms within which it was cast. The building encompassed 337 housing units.*

3. *A 1955 photograph which graphically demonstrates the devastation of bomb damage around St Paul's Cathedral and also the lost opportunity for a planned and harmonious rebuilding scheme.*

4

6

5

7

4. *Few public building projects were of the quality of Le Corbusier's Marseilles project, and this early British block is typical of the period.*

5. *The devastation left by wartime bombing meant that a new London arose in often bizarre juxtaposition with the old. The curtain wall construction techniques of the International Style meant that it was often from the residue of earlier buildings rather than from the new that cities retained their individuality.*

6. *Built under the London local administrative body of the time, the LCC, the Roehampton housing estate, which provided living accommodation for 10,000 people, consisted of two phases: the east, illustrated here and completed in 1959, was formed of post-Corbusier blocks, while the west, completed in 1955, consisted of four-storey maisonettes and two- and three-storey housing.*

7. *The enfants terribles of post-war British architecture, Peter and Alison Smithson, who rejected the Swedish Humanist school in favour of post-Corbusier New Brutalism. Their school at Hunstanton, built between 1949 and 1954, is regarded as the first example of this style, in which even electrical conduiting and plumbing were left exposed.*

NEW HORIZONS

1. The calm before the storm! Britain's first motorway, the M1, receiving a final brush before being opened in 1959. Having decimated the extensive Victorian-built railway network in favour of road building, planners underestimated the volume of traffic that roads would have to bear. Thirty years later they are still trying to get it right.

2. Eero Saarinen's mastery of sweeping concrete may be seen at Dulles International Airport, USA. As railway stations had been to an earlier age, airports were, in many ways, the major manifestations of fifties architecture.

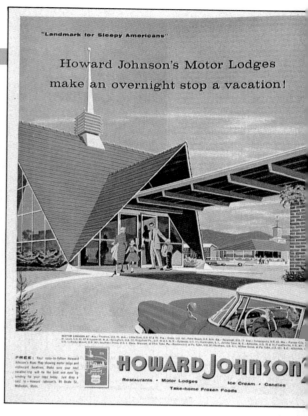

3. Now there were so many cars, roadside accommodation developed from the somewhat sleazy post-war motels to new, bright buildings, often featuring kitsch, commercial architecture, now often referred to as 'googie' architecture.

4. Britain's Gatwick Airport managed to avoid any form of architectural or design distinction.

MODERNISM

1. In 1984 the American Institute of Architects gave Mies van der Rohe and Philip Johnson's bronze and glass Seagram Building, New York (1956-8), its 25 year award, stating that it set the 'standard against which all modern steel architecture is measured'.

2. Lever House, New York (1952) was designed by Gordon Bunshaft of Skidmore, Owings and Merrill. It is regarded as the first commercial application of the concepts of Mies van der Rohe, or, as Tom Wolfe describes it, 'the mother of all the glass boxes'. Noteworthy for occupying only a quarter of its site, the rest being open plazas, it is designated an historical monument by the Landmark Preservation Commission of New York.

3

4

5

4. The Chapel of Notre Dame, Ronchamp, Haute Saône (1950-55) was Le Corbusier's first non-secular project. The dominant concrete roof has been described as 'visual acoustics'.

6

3. Known also for his work in industrial design (he founded Domus magazine), Gio Ponti is the most internationally renowned Italian architect. The Pirelli Office Block, Milan (1957-60), designed with the structural engineer Pier Luigi Nervi, is regarded as a masterpiece, with its distinctive tapering sides and delicate construction.

5. Alvar Aalto is another architect-designer. His architectural work, both in his native Finland and in the United States, combined advanced aesthetics with humanism in a unique manner. Illustrated here is Baker House, the dormitory block of the Massachusetts Institute of Technology.

6. Marcel Breuer had already made design history as head of the furniture department of the Bauhaus in the 1920s before he began working as an architect in the United States. His best known work was the UNESCO buildings in Paris, which he co-designed. Illustrated is the façade of St John's University (1953-61).

CONQUEST OF SPACE

1. Brasilia was built on virgin land in Brazil as a totally new city. It was the realisation of a futuristic vision and partly resulted from the profound influence of Le Corbusier on Brazilian architecture. Freed of the usual restraints of building on the confined sites of already established cities, the architect, Oscar Niemeyer, was able to emphasise the spatial relationships of the elements of his National Congress building. He is also famed for his Brazilian Pavilion at the 1939 New York World Fair.

2. The Brussels Expo of 1958 was a showcase of current design. The electronics firm Philips commissioned Le Corbusier to design their pavilion. The peaked mass of the entrance, seen here, shows the same dynamic upward thrust as his earlier church of Notre Dame du Haut.

3. The sweeping roofline of Eero Saarinen's Ingalls Hockey Rink at Yale University (seen here), together with the TWA building and Dulles Airport building are the culmination of his work. He died in 1961. There is still controversy as to whether these dramatic enclosures of space amount to more than one man's personal vision.

4. The Palazzetto dello Sport in Rome (1957) by Pier Luigi Nervi. This architect, a master of combining pure engineering with expressive aesthetics, had a philosophy of 'strength through form' which was realised in a series of space-spanning structures.

5

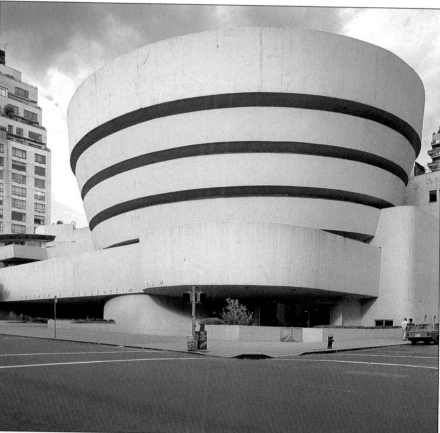

6

7

5 & 6. The Guggenheim Museum, New York, was designed by Frank Lloyd Wright between 1943-6, although actual construction occurred a decade later. The spiral ramp structure can be seen as the architect's self-indulgence, the fulfilment of his aborted 1925 design for a planetarium. He knew that this 'snail' construction would be controversial: 'They're going to try and figure this one out for years to come' was his comment. However after his death the museum was obliged to modify the gallery space to make it more practical.

7. Frank Lloyd Wright's Marin County Building, California, was one of his final projects. Although the contribution to architecture of the later works of his career is still being assessed, this vast structure, designed when he was nearly ninety, can be seen as symptomatic of the architectural conquest of space that characterised the fifties.

GLASS WALLS

1

2

1. The concept of open-plan offices emanated from the Bauhaus, where it was part of a democratic philosophy of an equal work environment. Mies van der Rohe paid lip service to the philosophy but compromised by re-introducing demarcation by means of different qualities of furniture and fittings. Eventually open space became a style that was as much about status and prestige as any other, as for example this architect's design for an entrance lobby.

2. The patio furniture of this Illinois house shows the easy transformation from indoor to outdoor living that characterised the open look.

3. The structural engineering that allowed open building was rarely put to full use. Rather, it engendered an attitude to living space that, before the excesses of consumerism finally triumphed, made for aesthetic simplicity.

4. Although Philip Johnson's House is best known for its totally glass walled, open look, it is sometimes forgotten that it must be seen in conjunction with the adjacent brick house that, in contrast, is enclosed for total privacy.

5. Although the idea of incorporating the garage into the living area never caught on (carbon monoxide fumes proving unconductive to elegant living), the car port extended the house to incorporate the beloved automobile.

DREAM HOMES

National HOMES invites you to the new "Ranger" open house showings...

NATIONAL HOMES CORPORATION
Lafayette, Indiana
Dept. L454

1. The demand for housing in the new suburban developments that mushroomed across the United States during the forties and fifties created a need for easily built and prefabricated units.

2. Home ownership became a reality for more young couples than ever before as changing social patterns opened up the new consumer market.

3. New suburbs were often 'little boxes made of ticky-tacky'. An essential feature was the undivided front lawn, for the etiquette of suburban living deemed fences to be unneighbourly.

4. Pink flamingos on the lawn represent the ultimate in American kitsch, and although screening the picture window against the sun was acceptable, it was generally left open, so that neighbours could monitor the decor.

5. The old suburbs, such as this in Rhode Island, mellowed in a way that could not be emulated by the new, with their almost identical houses, usually put up by speculative builders who bulldozed sites flat, clearing trees and landscape features as they went.

Alliance Graphique style poster by Tom Eckersley for the Post Office, 1951.

CHAPTER FOUR

COURTING

THE

CONSUMER

'SINCERITY IS THE QUALITY THAT COMES THROUGH ON TELEVISION.'

RICHARD NIXON, 1955

INTRODUCTION

Throughout the fifties the changes that were occurring in consumer lifestyles were reflected in marketing, packaging and advertising. The growth of interest in popular travel and tourism, for example, meant that travel posters, which had previously so tended to reflect the elitist elegance of international travel that art deco is sometimes called Liner style, now became bright, simple and often humorous. The work of artists from the Alliance Graphique International, particularly posters for Air France by Jean Picart le Doux and for the Swiss Tourist Authority by Pierre Monnerat, reflected this change. Another member of the Alliance, Eckersley in Britain, brought the same qualities to Guinness advertisements. Another change was the increase in do-it-yourself. Tools such as electric drills came to be packaged to appeal to the layman rather than the tradesman.

Although records had sometimes been packaged in decorative sleeves or boxes in the forties, the introduction of the vinyl LP and EP led to the development of a new graphic genre, the record sleeve. The genre was further extended with the advent of rock-and-roll. Now the graphics style had to appeal to teenagers and to reflect the image of the music; an early example of this, still regarded as a classic, is Elvis Presley's first LP. Other examples of the influence of the teenage market were soft drinks. Coca-Cola had featured teenagers in its advertisements in the forties, but these were now specifically targetted towards the young - 'Pepsi, for those who think young.'

Radios, record players, teen magazines, cosmetics and clothes (which included a new generation of girls' undergarments, particularly the pre-teen 'trainer' bra) were advertised as essentials for the teenage market. American advertising agencies were particularly alert to the conditioning of the young, establishing an attitude towards consumerism that would produce an even greater harvest with adulthood. Some stores even went so far as to introduce junior credit cards. This targetting of the young consumer was fostered in an environment where indulgence was endorsed by psychology (from the teachings of Dr Spock to the image of the misunderstood, under-privileged juvenile delinquent) and was seen as socially desirable.

Not only did a teen market appear. There was a trend to a 'young' image. In England *Punch* lost its Victorian look and used a colourful cartoon on the front covers. New magazines appeared, most significantly *Jet*, a sort of *Life* for the Black community, and, what was to become the most obvious example of lifestyle marketing, *Playboy*, which, at 50 cents, was relatively expensive but featured high-quality printing, as well as the centre fold, the first of which featured Marilyn Monroe. Colour reproduction was now extensively used in even cheap publications, and a mass of detective thrillers and science-fiction stories proliferated, in both paperback and magazines. The pop scene brought a range of teen-mags, and television encouraged listing magazines, such as *T.V. Guide*, while writers of a new zany type of satire found a popular market with *MAD* magazine.

ADVERTISING MAKES ITS MARK

The greatest increase in graphics during the fifties was in advertising. Billboard art was revived. In Europe it was used to cover the hoardings surrounding bomb sites and rebuilding works; in the United States it adorned the highways, reaching the vastly increased number of motorists. In turn, the increased numbers of automobiles created further advertising. The increase in road-related services brought a proliferation of catering, service stations and motels, all of which adopted, symbols and housestyles that could be instantly recognised by the motorist. Prime examples are Howard Johnsons, or McDonalds 'Golden Arches'. Greater motoring, and higher speeds also resulted in a profusion of direction and route signs.

The demand for instant recognition was not limited to motoring. As traditional stores declined in favour of supermarkets, packaging, which combined with advertising to allow the product to sell itself, became an essential key to marketing. Many products that had hitherto been sold loose over the counter, such as biscuits, flour and confectionary goods, now had to be packaged.

The move towards modern packaging had begun in the thirties, when Ben Nash carried out what is regarded as pioneer research into technical aspects of packages and market psychology. In 1935 the Container Corporation of America was formed, with Herbert Bayer as consultant. In 1952 the Package Designers' Council was organised to

2. As the automobile became increasingly important, new landmarks sprang up, their eye-catching appearance and instantly recognisable corporate logos an essential feature in attracting the motorist.

1. The use of the 'billowing skirt' scene from The Seven Year Itch *in the movie's publicity has made the image one of the era's most enduring ones. Both the simplistic lower case lettering of the main title and the neon-style script of the stars' names are period graphic devices, here put to effective use.*

1

It's great to "go steady" with this

cool, clean taste!

Here's the drink that's fun to be with—it has such a *sparkling personality!* Seven-Up fairly tingles your thirst away—with a flavor that's naturally cool and clean when you finish the bottle. The c-o-o-l, clean taste leaves your mouth feeling refreshing and full of tang. No stickiness—no come-back thirst. But take your time with 7-Up. Relish it. It's much too good to hurry with. For a really "cool" date, whether you're out with the crowd, or home with the books, make yours 7-Up. P. S. Try it with that hamburger next time. It's the greatest!

Watch "Soldiers of Fortune" for exciting TV adventure!

7up

Nothing does it like Seven-Up!

You like it...
it likes you!

2

3. Soft drink sales soared as teenagers had money to spend. Although juke box manufacturers disassociated themselves from the teenage market with its unwelcome associations of rock-and-roll and, by implication, juvenile delinquency, 7-Up continued its 'steadies' theme but with the contemporary leisure icon of the Rock-ola.

3

achieve recognition of package design as an integral factor in the consumer chain. By that time packaging was being subjected to two further influences: television and the increased use of plastics. Not only did television promote brand names, but the products themselves had to look visually stimulating in the advertisement, and, of course, it was often the packages rather than the products that were shown. Whether it was washing powder, an air freshener or a deodorant, the package, in effect, became the product. An extreme example of this was Old Forrester, which was advertised in 1955 for its bottle: 'the decanter sensation of the year designed by world-famous Raymond Loewy.' So closely was Coca-Cola identified with its bottle, which Loewy had restyled without detracting from its instantly recognisable lines, that it was originally available in cans only for overseas military installations.

The fifties was a great time for products being presented in a new manner. Anchovy paste came from toothpaste-type tubes; dessert toppings were squeezed from the new aerosols (an appropriate addition to the push-button kitchen); coffee was instant. Despite these high-tech packages, products were shown as user-friendly with bright, but by modern standards, crude, graphics.

Product endorsement, either by association or directly, was another way of humanising marketing, so the consumer had the assurances of such diverse characters as Bob Hope, Marilyn Monroe and Ronald Reagan, as well as of sports personalities, retired army generals and politicians. Other personalities marketing products became household names. Betty Furness was associated with Westinghouse Refrigerators and Betty Crocker with food mixes. Up-market products, on the other hand, divorced themselves from crude advertising by using famous artists. Elizabeth Arden commissioned Jean Cocteau, and Westraco commissioned Joan Miró, but the closest link between the fine and decorative arts was the Elgin American Bird in Hand powder compact, designed and endorsed by Salvador Dali.

FINE ART IN THE WORLD OF COMMERCE

During the fifties embryo fine artists were working in the commercial field. Although this in itself was not unprecedented (for example, Man Ray), a new development was the incorporation of commercial technique and images into fine art that is associated with Pop Art. Andy Warhol, high priest of the movement, worked as a commercial artist in New York from 1950 and in 1957 was awarded the Art Director's Club Medal for shoe advertisements. James Rosenquist, who worked as a billboard artist, stated: 'I read the billboard image as it is. I paint it as a reproduction of other things.'

The increased public awareness of modern art resulted in the plagiarism of fine art images and forms. Commonly found graphic devices were the elliptical form, which was derived from Alexander Calder, and the palette motif, which emanated from the Paris Montmartre look and which was found in textiles and furniture. Other recurring motifs were the angular lines of Buffet and the bright patches of colour of Matisse.

ART AND TECHNOLOGY

Stimulus also came from technology. The growth of the television culture produced a short-lived craze for TV-derived graphics, including not only the shape of the screen itself, but of wavy lines and the linear forms of television aerials. Jet travel produced the vapour trail line, and space and flying saucers were also popular images: 'Rock-and-roll, sputniks, flying saucers, now Edsel.' Oldsmobile ran a whole series of advertisements exploiting the associations of its Rocket models of the early fifties.

Colour fads came and went. One of the most widespread was the chlorophyll craze of the early fifties, when breath fresheners, chewing gum, deodorants and toothpaste all went green. The magic ingredient, which even found its way into dog food, was incorporated into over 90 products until the American Medical Association pointed out that, despite a diet full of the stuff, goats still smelled bad. Pink also enjoyed a boom for a while as colour became increasingly significant in advertising, even for such traditionally male-orientated items as cars, which became increasingly aimed at women.

This was the height of the consumer boom, when free, indiscriminate spending was the economic doctrine of the age. When the American economy went into recession in 1957, President Eisenhower was asked what the citizens

1. Oldsmobile ran a prolonged advertising series for its Rocket 88, a car that inspired the rhythm and blues song named after it. The Rocket, before the sinister associations of the word with nuclear war, was a popular symbol of futurism and progress.

2

2. Pink was the colour that symbolised modernity and fun - whether it was Elvis Presley's Cadillac, the hitherto conservative world of men's business wear, kitchen appliances or furnishings. Here, the new freedom from kitchen chores is promoted.

1

See Britain by Train

should do. 'Buy,' he replied. 'Buy what?' he was asked. 'Buy anything.'

Consumerism was similarly endorsed by British prime minister Harold MacMillan, whose claim in 1959 that 'you've never had it so good', epitomised the age. By the end of the decade, however, the pressures of marketing, including the confusion of special offers, 'own brands' and various configurations of packaging had led to a disenchantment with the advertising and marketing industries. Vance Packard's exposé of the techniques of selling to the affluent society anticipated the fair packaging legislation of the sixties, and the heady days of the first generation of mass-consumer advertising were over by the end of the fifties.

4

3. Abram Games' 1951 poster 'See Britain by train' has an almost Surrealist quality. In contrast, advertisements from the same campaign that were aimed at tourists from abroad and that appeared in magazines, were of a more traditional nature.

4. John Bainbridge's 1960 poster for BEA (British European Airways) exemplifies 'fine' graphic design.

INFLUENCES

1

2

Finishing Touch

An American Mustang pilot has latched himself onto the tail of a new Nip Navy plane—the Tojo. The frantic Jap has pulled every trick in the book. Finally, in desperation he racks his Tojo into a back-breaking 180 degree vertical turn. The Mustang pilot refusing to give up his advantage, follows. Halfway around the Mustang has out-turned the Tojo. At the three-quarter mark the Jap has turned into the gun sights of the Mustang. The American pilot applies the "finishing touch."

North American Aviation *Sets the Pace*

PLANES THAT MAKE HEADLINES ... the P-51 Mustang fighter (A-36 fighter-bomber), B-25 and PBJ Mitchell bomber, the AT-6 and SNJ Texan combat trainer. North American Aviation, Inc. Member, Aircraft War Production Council, Inc.

3

1. Post-war Britain experienced a revival of 'camp' Victorianism, and the riot of typography seen in this illustration of an early 19th-century hoarding, itself reminiscent of the landscape of the bombed cities, can be regarded as the forerunner of the bold, informal fifties look.

2. The circus, funfairs and music hall, officially recognised in the 'pop' element of the Festival of Britain, were traditional exponents of the colourful and zany imagery that were seen in product advertising.

3. The images of war persisted throughout the decade, in film, in graphics and in comics, where they also went through an easy transformation into science-fiction 'space' adventures.

4. The products of Walt Disney can be seen as the earliest international 'pop', not only in the animated films but also in the authorised use of characters to market countless items of merchandise, a concept pioneered by Disney. The care taken by the Studio to ensure that there was no deviation in the depiction of characters when they were used on these products set a high standard, which, coupled with improvements in printing technology, resulted in a better quality of packaging and display graphics.

5. The rise of the self-service supermarket in the late forties and fifties, coupled with TV advertising, transformed packaging. Now there was no sales clerk to recommend the product, manufacturers had to rely on presentation to ensure that it was their item that the shopper picked up.

6. The mobiles by Alexander Calder (1898-1976), exercises in spatial movement in the spirit of the atom Age, were echoed in graphic layouts and even the swing tickets that became a feature of product labelling.

PACKAGING

1. At a time when fast moving change was the norm, packaging often revitalised a product which was in itself perfectly conventional. Here the Philip Morris cigarette is advertised with the 'snap-open pack'. The box was designed by Raymond Loewy, whose studios were major contributors to new packaging.

2. As shopping patterns changed there was a greater reliance on self service so it became essential that packaging would match the promotion of goods through advertising and be instantly recognisable. Here the manufacturer's logo is given greater prominence than the product.

3. Market research discovered that products such as instant cake mix were acceptable to the consumer if presented in a homespun manner, to counteract the guilt women felt about shortcutting traditional skills. Reassuringly the cake on the pack does not betray its instant origins.

4. The less-than-interesting first aid dressing is subtly shown on its container in the guise of a banner (which also serves to illustrate the slogan 'Blends with your skin' by overlapping with the woman's arm). The overall impression is elegant, the presentation more usual for a fashion product.

1

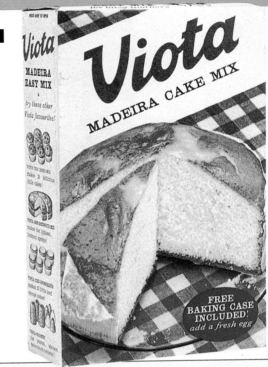

2

3

4

5. Self-service again influences, not only the prominent script of the name, but also the colour coding to identify each of the products in the range.

6. Traditional juvenile sweets, 'Dolly Mixtures', were given a bold, graphic presentation. In the past many sweets had been sold loose by weight, a practice that was eroded as small shops and personal service became scarcer.

7. Cereal packages such as this were cited by Design Sense magazine as 'a concrete symbol of the US marketing revolution.' Dynamic, eye-catching graphics were essential to market a

product aimed at 'junior'.
8. As packaging began to rival the actual product as the main selling point, care was taken to present the contents in a seductive manner. The illustration of these sweets makes full use of the advances made in colour printing.

NEON

1. Roadside signs proliferated over America as the country became more car orientated. Bowling, which had first become popular in the 1940s, now became a major leisure pursuit.

2. Las Vegas-style illumination developed into an unique art form, the most notable features of which were its garishness and large scale.

3. A by-product of the automobile culture was the range of car-orientated activities, including drive-in movies and, less commonly, drive-in churches. The drive-in eatery with its kitsch architecture, now known as 'googie', became a common sight.

4. Roadside graphics intruded into the American landscape in increasingly dramatic ways.

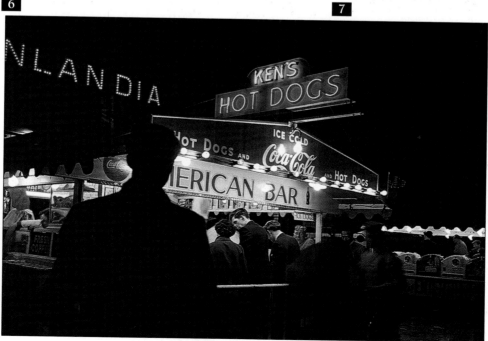

5

6

7

5. London's Battersea Pleasure Gardens and Fun Fair, originally a feature of the 1951 Festival of Britain, were the first major leisure grounds in Britain. Although many of the attractions were in the style of the traditional travelling fair, this 1952 picture captures something of the glamour the fair brought to drab, post-war London.

6. American influences, cocktails and jazz, had been seen in Britain during the twenties, but it was the war years that gave all things American a popular appeal. Even if it weren't called 'The American Bar', the hot dogs and Coca-Cola would reveal the cultural origins of this Blackpool fast-food stand.

7. Even in the 19th century, the cladding of buildings with advertising had been a feature of London. The large, animated neon displays of Piccadilly Circus, in themselves symbolic of a new age when they were switched on after the war-time blackout, became as much a landmark of the capital as the statue of Eros.

EXHIBITIONS

1. The Skylon, a 300-feet (91m) tower, was the most distinctive feature of the Festival of Britain. Unkind critics commented that its almost invisible means of support could be seen as symbolic of the state of the nation.

2. The Festival emblem was seen on a range of products as, briefly, the 'tonic to the nation' was seen to herald a new age.

5

4. Walt Disney's vision of the future, Tomorrowland, was a major attraction of Disneyland, California, when it opened in 1955. Shown here is the Carousel of Progress.

5. A 'Good Design' exhibition held in Chicago in 1952. Curved screens made of plastic string divided up the exhibits.

3

3. The main theme of the 1958 Brussels Expo was nuclear energy working for peace. This was reflected in the atomic structure of the main pavilion, which featured technical achievements of the decade.

4

1

2

1. Long before he started selling politics, Ronald Reagan was seen endorsing a variety of consumer products, including General Electric, Union Pacific Railroad and Chesterfield cigarettes. The mixture of several contrasting typefaces (often in the same sentence) in this advertisement is typical of the period, as are the small shots of heads to add authority to advertising claims.
2. Dale Robertson, star of the TV western Wells Fargo, endorsing an oil filter. The link between American television and advertising was so close that it seems natural even in a magazine advertisement. Animation and photography are mixed together unselfconsciously.

3. Camel cigarette advertisements had a long tradition of featuring personalities from the world of entertainment. Phil Silvers as the scheming Sergeant Bilko was one of television's most popular figures. The final slogan is hand-lettered. There was great interest in calligraphy from graphic designers.

4. Rock Hudson gives an air of elegance to Eagle clothes. The very realistic illustration has been based on a photograph. This halfway house between photography and illustration was common practice.

5. The glamour-by-association ploy is explicit when the manufacturers of Lustre-Creme Shampoo can claim that it is the 'favorite beauty shampoo of four out of five top Hollywood stars' - particularly when Marilyn Monroe is one of them!

BOOKS AND RECORDS

A.E. Van Vogt

LE MONDE DES A

Le Rayon Fantastique

1

(Penguin) **Penguin Plays**

CAT ON A HOT TIN ROOF

Tennessee Williams

2/6

2

1. In an age that produced a wave of flying saucer sightings and was to close with the actual exploration of space, science fiction enjoyed increased popularity and images of spaceships and aliens abounded. This illustration dates from 1953.

2. The publishing house Penguin, which had popularised paperback literature, abandoned its standardised covers in favour of more innovative graphics.

3. Hearts, *featuring Jayne Mansfield, was typical of a range of pulp publications.*

4. *Elvis Presley's first LP brought about a new style of rock graphics, which characterised his subsequent records.*

5. *Although jazz records were normally presented with enigmatic abstracts or moody, stark photography, this Kai Winding LP sleeve is in the same mode as the period's casual advertisements.*

MAGAZINES AND COMICS

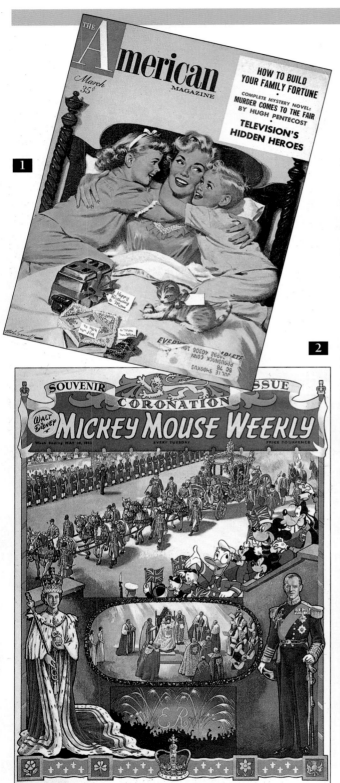

1. The traditional family image portrayed for an American magazine. The beribboned electrical toaster is typical of a time when small domestic appliances were extensively advertised as being suitable gifts, welcomed, in theory at least, by women as freeing them from domestic chores.

2. There is an almost pop-art quality about the combination of two cultures in the Mickey Mouse Weekly coronation souvenir issue. Many Britons considered the commercial exploitation of the event, particularly by American television, to be inappropriate.

3. Flying saucers and UFOs became part of the folklore of the decade after a US pilot reported seeing nine saucer-like objects in the sky near Washington in 1947. During the fifties an average of six hundred sightings a year were reported, and the US Air Force spent an annual $60,000 investigating.

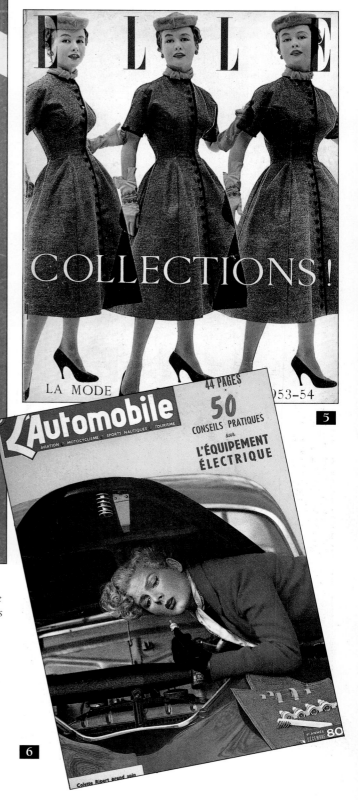

4. This 1957 cover of Time serves as a reminder of the dark side of the era. The shadow of the bomb meant that any conflict could threaten world peace, and this fear, in turn, generated an atmosphere of escapism.

5. Elle demonstrates French elegance in this arresting graphic presentation of 1953.

6. Practical advice on automobile electrical equipment from 1951 is given an appeal it might otherwise have lacked. Nevertheless, as the number of women drivers increased, automobile manufacturers could no longer feature women simply as decoration in advertising aimed at men, especially as women's evening classes in car maintenance became popular.

SELLING CORPORATIONS

1. The enormous growth in civil aviation can be seen in this display of airline logos.

2. By 1955, when John Bainbridge designed this poster for British European Airways, post-war austerity had given way to consumerism. The figure of Britannia, whose 19th-century use had been revived for the Festival of Britain, is given a pop treatment, almost anticipating the 'swinging London' imagery of the next decade.

3

4

5

3. The stylized Britannia, designed by Abram Games as the official symbol of the 1951 Festival of Britain, appeared on everything from postage stamps to novelty souvenirs.

4. Readily identifiable graphics became essential roadside landmarks, as shown by this Howard Johnson's at Albany, New York.

5. The British Design Centre endorsed products that satisfied its sometimes erratic criteria. Those items were allowed to display this sign.

POSTERS

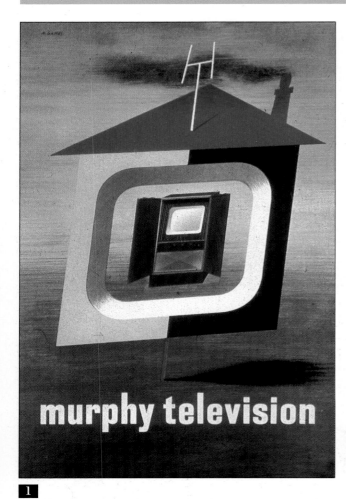

1. Abram Games, best known for his Festival of Britain graphics, combines the fifties interest in typography with the surrealist humour of the period in this 1951 ad.

2. John Bainbridge's 1953 'posterise and publicise' exploits the advances made in colour-printing technology.

3. French and Italian influences were seen not only in the techniques and subject matter of films but also in the presentation.

4. Rock-and-roll movie graphics, soon to become stereotyped, were, on the whole, simplistic in their determination to capture the energy of the music. The films themselves were generally low-budget affairs, aiming at exploiting what was seen as nothing more than an ephemeral craze, and their presentation usually reflects this attitude.

5. Although the science-fiction genre produced some of the most interesting films of the fifties, such as The Incredible Shrinking Man (1957), the low-budget end of the market now attracts a cult following, fascinated by its period absurdities. The posters often bore little or no resemblance to actual scenes in the films and were more a form of pop folk art in their depiction of space fantasies.

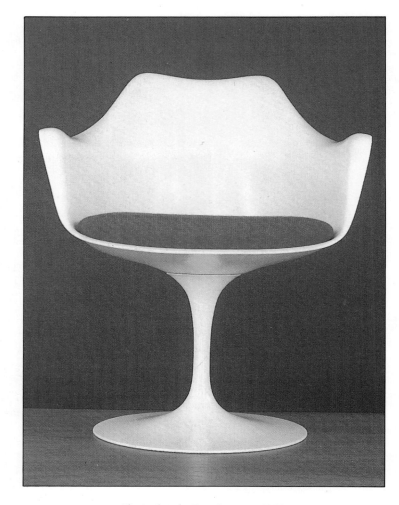

Plastic chair by Eero Saarinen, 1957.

CHAPTER FIVE

SUBURBIA GOES SPACE AGE

'IN THIS INCREASINGLY MECHANIZED CIVILIZATION OUR HOMES ARE THE ONLY REMAINING PLACE FOR PERSONAL EXPRESSION.'

MARY AND RUSSEL WRIGHT,
GUIDE TO EASIER LIVING, 1950

INTRODUCTION

1

1. Linear spatial structures were a recurring theme in sculpture and furniture design as well as in graphic motifs (as in this textile design).

2. The ingredients of modern furnishing were indiscriminately juxtaposed in an attempt to create 'contemporary' decor. The result is merely to achieve a bleaker version of the traditional sitting room.

Many factors combined to influence the great proliferation of domestic design that characterised the post-war period and the fifties. The destruction of war and the shifts of populations, either directly or indirectly related to the war, created a massive boom in building and an equal demand for furniture and consumer durables. The 'Blue Skies' visions of the future had, as we saw in Chapter 1, fostered a climate that favoured modernity, and this coincided with a new-found capacity for mass production, often utilising techniques that had been developed during the war.

FURNISHING THE OPEN PLAN

The traditional concept of the home also changed in the immediate post-war period, particularly as designated interior space declined in favour of open-plan schemes.

This was partly the result of new construction methods, which made obsolete the need for internal load-bearing walls, and partly the result of a greater informality of lifestyle combined with a desire for spaciousness. There was also a widely held feeling of flexibility and impermanence. No longer did people save to buy furnishings that would last a lifetime. Rather, generally increased affluence, with a trend towards earlier marriage, and a collective sense that the near future would result in betterment - higher standards of living, 'newer' designs, improved technology - all combined to encourage consumers to what furniture that was both 'modern' and expendable.

At the same time, many designers - even those not directly working in the popular market - began to adopt the techniques and materials of mass production. Despite the pre-war influence of the Bauhaus, modern furniture and lighting had been largely the domain of fine art deco or had been debased commercial copies. The United States had, for instance, seen most of its own furniture manufacturers at the higher level of the market losing out to European imports, and a lowering of standards in its own products at the lower levels. An exception was the Herman Miller Company, which in the thirties commissioned furniture by Gilbert Rohde, the major American Modernist of the time. The furniture attracted wide publicity at the 'Century of Progress' Exhibition in Chicago in 1933, and within a year Herman Miller dropped its traditional range in favour of Rohde's designs. In 1946, following Rohde's death, George Nelson took over and expanded the range to include designs by Charles Eames and Isamu Noguchi.

Although at this time Herman Miller was the only major company, not only in the United States but in the world, to

ART & DÉCORATION
la revue de la maison
fondée en 1897

N° 46
1955
390 f.

3

be exponents of Modernism, another important contributor was beginning to emerge. Hans Knoll left Germany, where his father, a furniture manufacturer, had known Walter Gropius and had made pieces for the Bauhaus in 1937. Another European, the Dane Jens Risom, who had arrived in New York at about the same time, began to design furniture for Knoll. Together they designed and built the press lounge for the General Motors Pavilion and a kitchen for the America at Home section of the 1939 New York World's Fair.

By the end of the forties, Knoll Associates included Charles Eames, Alvar Aalto, Hans Wegner, Abel Sorensen, Harry Bertoia, Mies van der Rohe and Eero Saarinen. Risom ceased to be associated with Knoll, and founded his own group, Jens' Risom Design, which specialised in wood furniture. In 1941 the Museum of Modern Art exhibited the results of its competition, Organic Design in Home Furnishing, in which Saarinen and Eames had won first prize for a moulded plywood chair based on the techniques of forming plywood that Charles Eames and his wife, Ray (Ray Kaiser), had been perfecting since the late thirties, and that had already achieved fame through Ray's designs for plywood splints for the US Navy.

The success of this competition led to the Museum of Modern Art running a competition in 1946 for printed fabrics, and this was followed in 1948 by the Low Cost Furniture Design, the main criterion of which was that not only should the items satisfy the low cost element but that no awards would be given until the items were actually in production. The judges described the furniture they were looking for; it had 'to serve the needs of the vast majority of people; furniture that is planned for small apartments and homes; furniture that is well designed yet moderate in price, that is comfortable but not bulky, and that can be easily moved, stored and cared for; in other words, furniture that is integrated to the needs of modern living and production.' Among the winners were Charles Eames, with a version of the Saarinen-Eames plywood chair of 1941 but designed to be produced in fibre-glass, and Robin Day and Clive Lattimer for storage units.

In 1951 *Life,* in a feature entitled 'Modern Living', could show 26 pieces of furniture (for dining room, living room, bedroom and child's room) with a total retail price of only $1,800 ('modern furniture comes in a bargain priced package') all designed by Eames and George Nelson for the Herman Miller Company. The article explained that the Eames plywood chair, for example, consisted of 17 pieces, all machine made, that could be produced in only three hours. The only hand assembly required was to fix the seat and the back. The chair, stronger than a traditional one, sold for $29. In contrast, a traditional chair had up to a hundred components, was labour intensive, took about 10 hours to make and sold for $50.

3. This mid-fifties kitchen demonstrates how the room is now seen not only as functional but as stylish in its own right. Domestic appliances were in the forefront of consumer marketing, the newest design in kitchen equipment being second only in advertising terms to the latest model car.

4. Although the natural properties of wood tended to dominate Scandinavian and, to an extent British, design, new materials and techniques were widely regarded as freeing the designer, as in this French dressing-table in Formica laminate.

The most popular chair, however, was of even simpler construction than the Eames version. The Hardoy chair was a simple frame, of welded mild steel rod, over which a canvas envelope was slung. Although Knoll had acquired the production rights in the late forties, it was an easy design to fabricate and was much copied. The chair's exact origins were clouded in confusion, and in 1950 it was held to be public property. Not only were these chairs cheap, comfortable and topical, they satisfied the current aesthetic of furniture as sculpture.

A classic example of spatial furniture is the chicken wire chairs of Harry Bertoia. Bertoia had trained as an architect and as a silversmith, and he regarded his chairs as practical sculpture: 'The chairs are studies in space, form and metal too. If you will look at them you will find that they are mostly made of air, just like sculpture. Space passes right through them.' They were also exercises in practical design, too, for in the 'better mousetrap' tradition, Bertoia commented: 'The urge for good design is the same as the urge to go on living. The assumption is that somewhere, hidden, is a better way of doing things.'

DESIGNS FOR LIVING

An example of the close links between sculpture and design of that period can be seen in the work of Isamu Noguchi, a Japanese American, whose career included working under Gutzon Borglum (sculptor of

4

1

1. The fabric designs of Marianne Straub demonstrate the uncompromising brashness that typifies the era.

2. Although the rest of the table features a conservative approach, the table mats show a practical use for decorative laminate offcuts. Popular magazines, encouraged by the increasing popularity of 'do-it-yourself', often gave home-improvement hints on utilising such items.

2

Mount Rushmore), studying medicine and working in Paris (on a Guggenheim Fellowship), China (where he studied calligraphy) and Japan (where he studied pottery). He was a controversial and colourful part of the New York art scene in the pre-war years. In 1945, having been voluntarily kept in a camp for alien Japanese through the war, an exhibition of his sculpture was held at New York City's Museum of Modern Art. In 1948 he designed a table lamp of translucent plastic, and in 1951 the Akari series of paper lamps, which were made for him in Japan. His influence can be seen in the bubble lamps that were designed by George Nelson and William Renwick for the Herman Miller Company. Using a technique developed during the war in which plastic film was sprayed to produce a translucent skin over a wire frame, these were a modern version of Japanese paper lamps.

Plastic was also used in a totally different way in the lighting design of Italy's Gino Sarfatti - a PVC shield could be adjusted to deflect light - and another of Sarfatti's designs consisted of hanging shallow, acrylic drums.

Another industrial technique that found a design application was that of metal spinning. Thin material, usually aluminium, was formed into concave shapes, a technique that had already been used for lamp designs in the metal workshop of the Bauhaus in the twenties, especially by Marianne Brandt. The technique was also commonly seen in photographers' studio lamps, which, in turn, were incorporated as 'high tech' lighting in domestic interiors.

In 1953, French designer Serge Mouille, who had carried out experimental work in alloys, including the production of a car body in Duralinox, began to work in lighting. In 1954 an article in *Décor d'Aujourd'hui* likened him to Calder in the way he interpreted natural form, such as shells, in aluminium, and in 1956 Galérie Steph-Simon mounted an exhibition of lighting by Serge Mouille and Isamu Noguchi.

The one lighting design that is most typical of the fifties, however, was not the work of a major designer. Rather it was the sort of practical gadget or novelty that was also typical of the spirit of the age - the pole or pogo lamp. This was basically a metal tube, each end of which was tipped with rubber springs, which enabled the tube to be jammed between the floor and ceiling. From the pole was suspended a cluster of small reflector lamps, which could be adjusted, making it one of the most flexible of lighting systems. Sometimes the pole also incorporated a small table. This was, in style terms, closely related to George Nelson's 1958 storage system, in which a framework of poles supported adjustable shelving.

A similar modular system was designed by Paul McCobb for the Mutschler Company. This system echoes the theme of flexibility which recurs at every point, and was the effect of two factors. The first was the idea of modular housing units, which had been proposed by, among others, Buckmaster Fuller. The second was pre-fabrication, another war-time development which had been seen in, for example, the Liberty Ships, and which was seen as the answer to fast house building, with the additional advantage that, as need arose, the house could be extended with further units.

PRE-FABRICATING THE FUTURE

In 1954 the Monsanto Company commissioned the Massachusetts Institute of Technology to develop a fibreglass pre-fabricated house. The result - four room units, each of two mouldings, the floor and lower walls, and the roof and upper walls - was built in 1957 by the same company that made plastic bodies for the Chevrolet Corvette and was installed, as the House of the Future, at Disneyland.

A similar idea of pre-fabricating a house was shown at London's Ideal Home Exhibition, 1956. This House of the Future, designed by architects Alison and Peter Smithson, was a plastic shell with no external windows but containing an inner courtyard with windows facing onto it. Flexibility was again the theme. For example, the dining table could sink into the floor when it was not in use, and the kitchen was almost non-existent, with cooking pans containing their own heating elements and so doing away with the cooker.

This sort of modernity was too optimistic: it took no account of building regulations and costs, and the latter were to be the main drawback to the use of pre-fabricated housing units in the United States - the development of the Monsanto House of the Future had cost over $1 million. But modernity at this level also negated the other major factor of the fifties - consumerism. Few people would be interested in a non-kitchen, for example. The ideal of the time was a fully modern kitchen that, in the favoured style of open plan, was not only integrated into the living areas but was also on public view. The kitchen was, in fact, a status symbol and was flaunted as such. As the site of the major concentration of consumer items in the home, the kitchen became the battleground of the marketing war. Appliance manufacturers began to introduce the same design obsolescence that characterised the automobile, including a range of fashion colours. Built-in kitchens, with appliances incorporated into a total design, which had begun to appear before the war, became the norm. Hotpoint was the leading applicance manufacturer to research designer kitchens, and the company established a Visual Design Department under Raymond Sandin to undertake a Custom Trend programme between 1954 and 1959. New ideas were subjected to market research, and as convenience foods, dishwashers and waste-disposal units helped to make the kitchen less environmentally intrusive, its incorporation into the home as a living area combined both the new ideal of the woman surrounded by sophisticated, push-button gadgetry and the

3

traditional, rural concept of the kitchen as the focal point of family life.

This ambiguity typifies much of the style of the age, for the desire for a world of tomorrow was, in reality, usually tempered by an atavistic preference for what were regarded as 'traditional' values. As the number of gadgets featured in the kitchen increased, the popularity of the patio barbeque increased, and that, of course, in turn produced a range of sophisticated barbeque gadgets. Similarly, the clean lines of the International Style interior became customised with real or imitation wood panelling and stone fireplaces. Houseplants, especially - with the introduction of sophisticated home heating and insulation - exotic tropicals, became both a symbol of modernity, with their sculptural qualities, and a humanising element. By the end of the decade the future had already arrived in the form of the sputnik, and the public was turning back from the truly modern to pseudo-modern.

3. The fifties, more than any period before, was the age when the design and furnishing of the home became an almost universal preoccupation, whether it was with designer articles or with the more mundane mass-produced items that nevertheless often attempted to capture the spirit of the modern look.

INFLUENCES

1   **2**

1. The bedroom of the experimental Bauhaus Am Horn house (1923) acts as a prelude to the fifties simplistic wood furniture, which characterised the Scandinavian look.

2. Jean (or Hans) Arp's painted relief The Forest (1916) features the colours and forms that were to appear in fifties furnishing fabrics.

3. The decade was dominated by a love-hate relationship with the atom. The sinister side was 'the Bomb', an object of constant dread. On the other hand, atomic power was seen as the key to a science-fiction future as celebrated at the Brussels Expo. The 'atom' ball and stick, echoed in the cherry-on-a-stick featured in cocktails, became a common design motif, the ball providing a logical cap to a variety of spindly metal structures.

4. Marcel Breuer's 1925 chair set a standard of spatial design that liberated furniture and allowed a series of design exercises in unconventional seating, which resulted in such pieces as the Hardoy, Bertoia and Eames chairs.

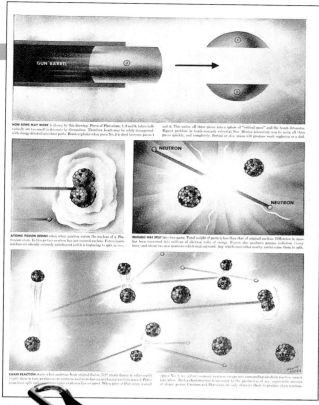

5. The aesthetics of Japanese interiors seemed close to the open-plan look. Raymond Loewy, who later acted as a design consultant for the Japanese government, built the St Tropez Villa in the Japanese style.

6. The interior of Frank Lloyd Wright's Falling Water house (1937) has textured wall surfaces, low ceilings and low furniture - all later characteristics of fifties interiors.

EUROPEAN DESIGN

3. Marcello Nizzoli, a major 20th-century Italian designer, is famous for his contribution to the Victory salon at the sixth Triennale in 1936 and his work with Olivetti, which he joined in the same year. He is known for graphic work and industrial design. This Miretta sewing-machine was designed for Nechi in 1956.

1. Eero Saarinen's tulip chairs of moulded fibreglass are regarded as timeless classics. His fluid, spatial sense is demonstrated here as well as in his architecture.

2. The Turin designer Carlo Mollino is best known for his organic-form furniture, some of which had its roots in Art Nouveau. Italian designers were less purist in the use of wood than the British and Scandinavian, and this desk has a formica laminate top.

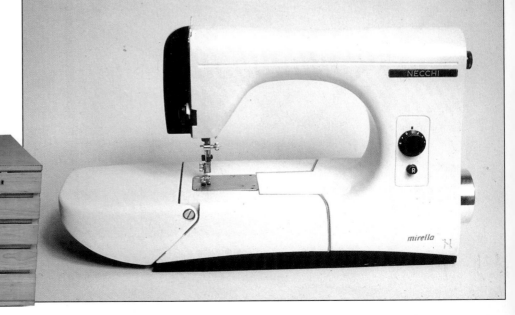

5

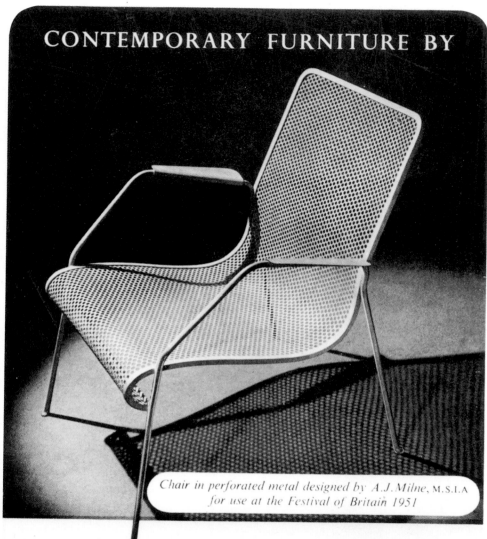

CONTEMPORARY FURNITURE BY

Chair in perforated metal designed by A.J. Milne, M.S.I.A for use at the Festival of Britain 1951

HEAL'S

HEAL & SON LTD 196 TOTTENHAM COURT ROAD W-

TELEPHONE: MUSEUM 1666   TELEGRAMS: FOURPOSTER · RATH · LONDO
(2nd Impression)

4. The Festival of Britain acted as a showcase for, and a patron to, British designs, such as this chair.

5. Mondrian-style shelving modules proved popular. This wood and lacquered aluminium unit is by Jean Prouve, Charlotte Periand and Sonia Delaunay.
6. Another example of the designs of Marcello Nizzoli, the Sapnat 217 telephone of 1958, with its clearly defined buttons and stylishly moulded plastic case, is characteristic of his work.

6

OPEN PLAN LIVING

1. Open plan, a concept that can be traced back to the beginning of the century, became increasingly popular, symbolising the more informal nature of domestic life. Here the bookcase in the foreground separates a living room area from a study area.

2. 1958's Ideal Home Exhibition showed this executive office. Although open-plan work environments were believed to produce more democratic and brighter working conditions, in practice the quality of furnishings and layout maintained demarcations of status.

3. Modular shelving units as dividers were a standard fixture of open plan, as was the vogue for using different wallpapers to define different areas of the house.

3

ALL ELECTRIC HOME

1 **2**

1 & 2. Electricity, which in some parts of Europe came into the home only during the decade, transformed domestic chores, as well as introducing the comfort of the electric blanket. Comparing the British advertisement above with the American one below indicates just how far ahead was US industrial design in terms of technology, style and choice. The elegantly attired lady operating her food mixer is a typical glossy image in the advertising of the period which stressed how modern appliances removed drudgery from household tasks.

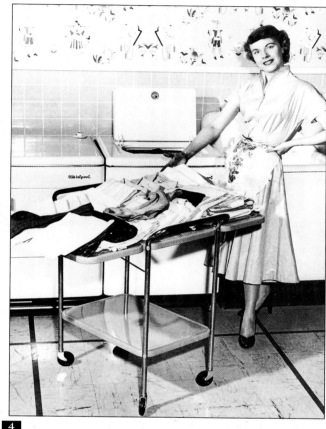

3. Although the fitted kitchen had been advocated since the forties, appliances remained as separate units until the late fifties, when they became fully integrated. This 1957 picture shows the test kitchen of the Electrical Association for Women in the UK.

4. The Whirlpool compact washer and automatic dryer represented the progress achieved in a decade that had begun with the washing machine as a luxury item and the clothes mangle a standard feature in many homes.

5. The Frigidaire 'kitchen of tomorrow' showed the innovative concept of eye-level refrigerator and freezer units.

SEATING DESIGN

1. Piero Fornasetti was an illustrator and designer who worked with Gio Ponti, to whom he introduced the possibilities of trompe-l'œil. Examples by Fornasetti shown here are the Theme and Variation metal table, guitar chairs and folding screen.

1

2. Architect/designer Charles Eames won, with Eero Saarinen, first prize in the Museum of Modern Arts' Organic Design in Home Furnishing Exhibition in 1940, and subsequently founded the furniture company Plyform Products. In 1948 Herman Miller started producing Eames' designs. Although mainly concerned with economy furniture, his most famous chair is an exception - in rosewood and leather, it was first designed for film director Billy Wilder.

3

3. The resin-bonding of plywood, developed in the forties, allowed for sophisticated forming techniques, the most important exponents of which were Charles and Ray Eames. Designed in 1950 by Carl Jacobs for Kandaga, these chairs demonstrate a utilitarian use of the material.

2

4. A laminated wood and metal chair by Piero Fornasetti. This designer's background is in theatre and painting. He was considered something of an outsider even in the fifties, taste now seems to be turning in his favour and there is a revival of interest in his work.

5. The American silversmith and sculptor Harry Bertoia designed these famous chickenwire chairs for Knoll Associates. The removable covers are generally considered to thwart their claim to be spatial sculpture. Although the chairs shown are in chrome, the originals were in black lacquer.

LIGHTING

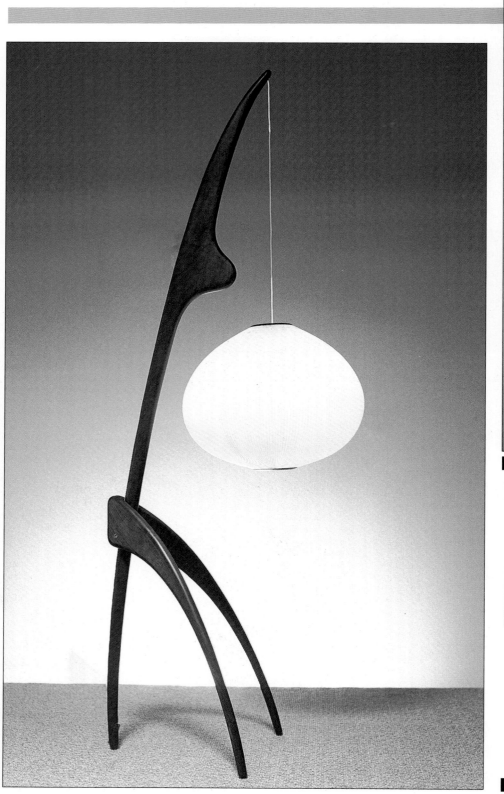

1. The Rispal 'tripod' lamp, in its use of organic wood form and Japanese style, shows the influence of Isamu Noguchi (b.1904). This design was later plagiarised in a debased commercial form.

2. The use of spun metal was a major element in lighting. This pendant lamp by Troughton & Young combines direct, diffused and reflected light.

5. *The table lamp by Pierre Guariche embodies the aesthetics of a delicate, minimalist structure that was then in vogue.*

6. *Designed in 1955 by Poul Henningsen for the Danish firm Louis Poulsen, this pendant light, of which there were several variations, remains a timeless classic. The colour was used to enhance the effect of the then white-painted, spun aluminium reflectors.*

3. *A conventional table lamp, designed by A.B. Rhead for the Poole Pottery Company, is in the same mode as vases and bowls in the company's range.*

4. *The Pogo lamp is a uniquely fifties concept, not only because of its 'arty' origins (it was reputedly improvised by a photographer from his studio lights), but because of its flexible use in open-plan living, sometimes being used in groups as room dividers. Some manufacturers even incorporated small tables into the design to increase its versatility.*

PATTERNS AND TEXTILES

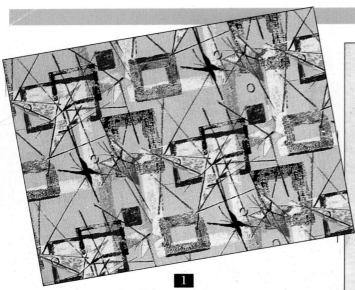

1

1. Abstract designs were popular, particularly as increased prosperity freed the consumer from the constraint of having to make furnishings last a lifetime.

2. Fabric transformed an otherwise unadventurous form into a 'contemporary' piece.

3. The London store, Heal's, had a long-established tradition of adopting new designs, such as these 1952 textiles.

2

3

Furnishing Textiles

CALYX *and* ALLEGRO, *designed by Lucienne Day* – LEAF & LINE *designed by Michael O'Connell*

HEAL'S
of London

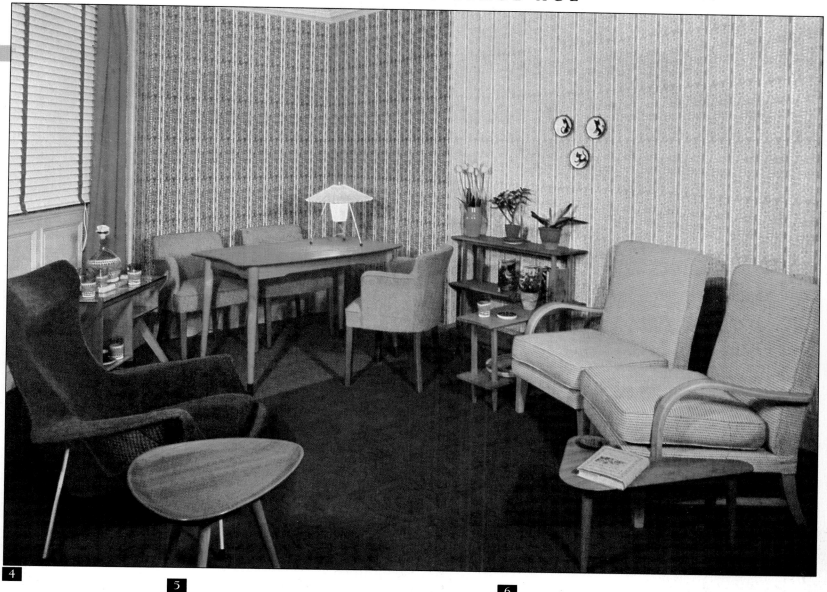

4

5

6

4. *The Daily Mail Ideal Home Book of 1951 featured this 'modern' room. The wallpaper pattern was Mexico, designed by Armfield Passano: different colour combinations were used to separate the dining area from the rest of the room.*

5. *This 1959 design, 'Leaves', was by Lily Goddard.*

6. *'Fruitcup' - almost an up-dated version of a William Morris pattern.*

KITSCH

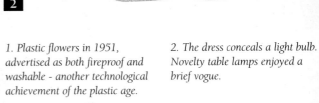

1. Plastic flowers in 1951, advertised as both fireproof and washable - another technological achievement of the plastic age.

2. The dress conceals a light bulb. Novelty table lamps enjoyed a brief vogue.

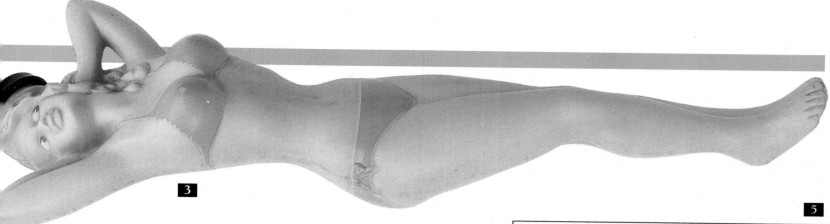

3

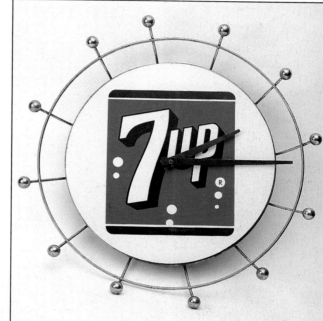

5

3. The cult of the 'pin-up' was often bizarre. This curvaceous young lady is, in fact, a hot-water bottle, the stopper being her pill-box hat. It is not known whether she was produced as a joke item or as a fantasy novelty.

4. This ingenious version of a draughtsman's aid exploited Marilyn Monroe's image as 'sex goddess'.

5. George Nelson's atom ball clock, now regarded as a classic design, spawned a host of imitations, including this advertising clock.

6. It is difficult to believe that anyone ever took this American plastic toaster cosy seriously, yet, despite the high-tech image of the age, these homely accessories were produced.

4

6

ATOMIC HOME

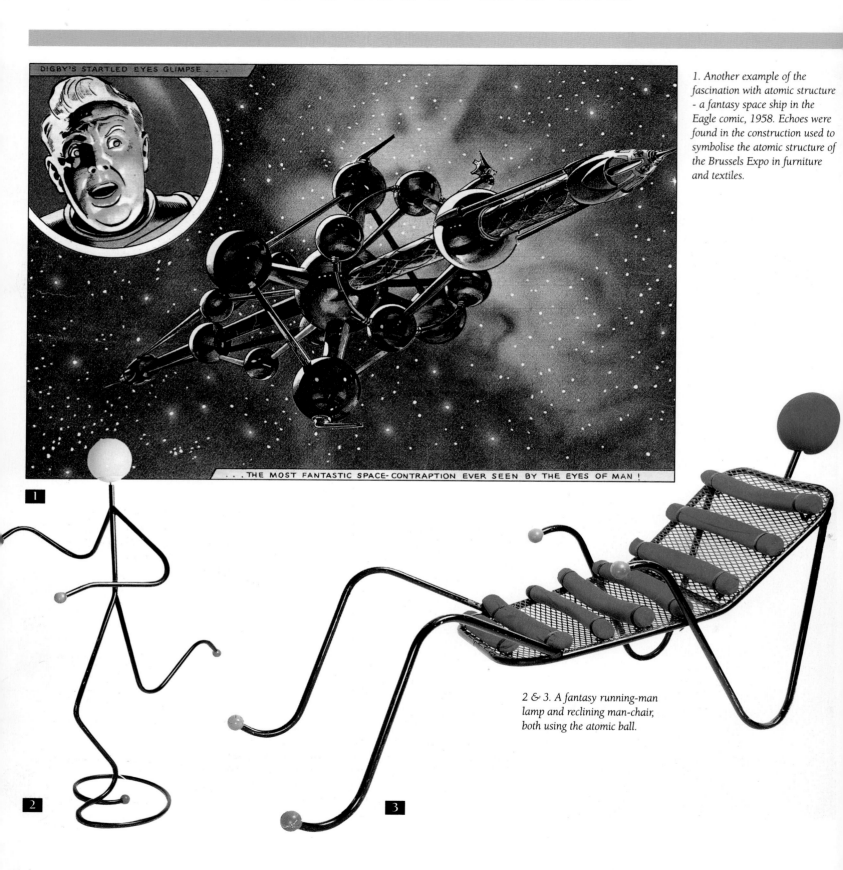

DIGBY'S STARTLED EYES GLIMPSE . . .

. . . THE MOST FANTASTIC SPACE-CONTRAPTION EVER SEEN BY THE EYES OF MAN !

1. Another example of the fascination with atomic structure - a fantasy space ship in the Eagle comic, 1958. Echoes were found in the construction used to symbolise the atomic structure of the Brussels Expo in furniture and textiles.

2 & 3. A fantasy running-man lamp and reclining man-chair, both using the atomic ball.

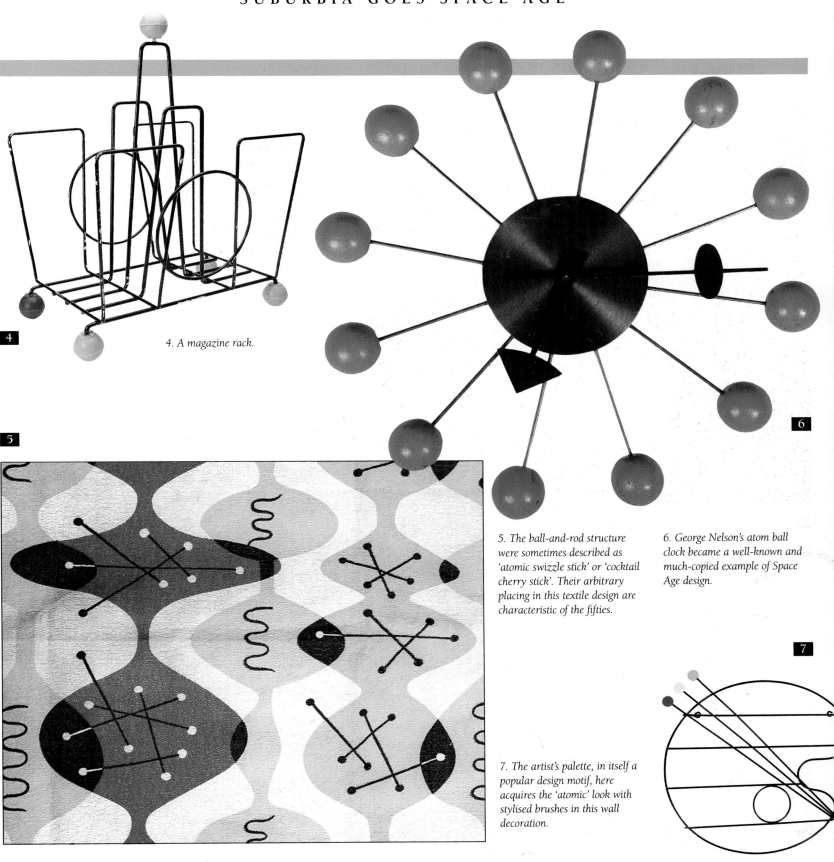

4. A magazine rack.

5. The ball-and-rod structure were sometimes described as 'atomic swizzle stick' or 'cocktail cherry stick'. Their arbitrary placing in this textile design are characteristic of the fifties.

6. George Nelson's atom ball clock became a well-known and much-copied example of Space Age design.

7. The artist's palette, in itself a popular design motif, here acquires the 'atomic' look with stylised brushes in this wall decoration.

CERAMICS AND GLASS

1. The Italian company Venini was in the forefront of a revival in glass production, at the same time finding new applications for such traditional techniques as lattacino (lace) decoration. Adventurous in the use of colour and form, Venini employed many important designers, most notably Fulvio Branconi and Riccardo Licata, designer, in 1956, of the Morandiane bottles.

2. Of equal stature to Venini was Barovier & Toso, another Italian glass company, which had been created by the amalgamation of Vetreria Artistica Barovier and Saiar Ferro Toso. The company's most distinctive designs utilised a unique technique of applying colour decoration while the glass was in its molten stage.

4

5

6

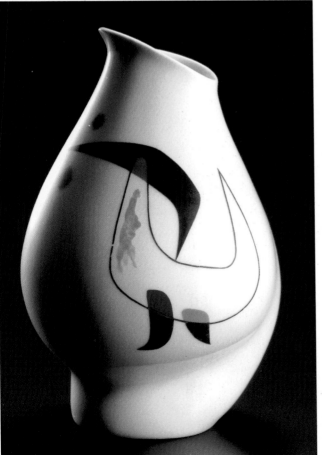

3. The influence of studio craft ceramics was seen in commercially produced pieces. Although, as this example shows, the fine quality and delicacy that characterised manufacturers such as Rosenthal continued, surface decoration to give a 'folksy' look, such as this woven effect, was popular.

4. The Como tea and coffee set in silver plated metal, designed by Lino Sabattini for the French firm Christofle (1956), is an extreme example of organic Modernism.

5. This vase from the Rosenthal Studio Line was designed by Fritz Heidenreich and decorated by Klaus Bendixen. The Studio Line was intended to bring 'great artists to your table' by commissioning important artists to decorate mass-produced ceramics. The most important contributor to the range was, perhaps, Jean Cocteau.

6. Britain's Poole Pottery Company was unusual in promoting new design at a time when the majority of the industry concentrated on traditional wares, which succeeded in the export market. This dish by Alfred Reade dates from 1953.

7. This cigarette lighter expressed both the popular organic form as well as being reminiscent of another popular motif, the artist's palette. Although true industrial design was changing the shape of everyday life, many items were being packaged or styled to give them a spurious 'modern' look.

INTO THE FUTURE

1

3

2

1, 2 & 3. Peter and Alison Smithson were major exponents of Modernist architecture in Britain, commissioned to design the House of the Future for the 1956 Daily Mail *Ideal Home Exhibition*. The house was an exercise in futurist design, built of pre-fabricated plastic. The Smithsons admired the manufacturing methods of the American auto industry. The mass production-based industries had already revolutionised half the house - the kitchen, bathroom, laundry room and garage. The architects advocated using factory-built, fitted kitchen units which could be easily updated. The House of the Future took the concept of flexibility beyond conventional open plan with only the kitchen and bathroom modules differentiated from the rest. An electrostatic dust collector was provided and cooking utensils incorporated their own heating elements. It was ideas such as these that impressed visitors to the exhibition rather than the building itself, with no external windows.

5. Disney's 'Tomorrowland', which opened in 1955 was more than a novelty theme park; it realised many schemes for the future. For example the elevated 'people mover' seen here gave the Federal government enough confidence to invest over seven million dollars in a feasibility study for an elevated system for San Francisco and a plastics firm spent over a million dollars on building the prefabricated plastic House of the Future.

4. The public had high expectations that the future would be brighter and better. In this rather prophetic exhibit at the Daily Mail *Ideal Home Exhibition* the television set, still a novelty in Britain, becomes part of the fireplace as the new focal point of the room.

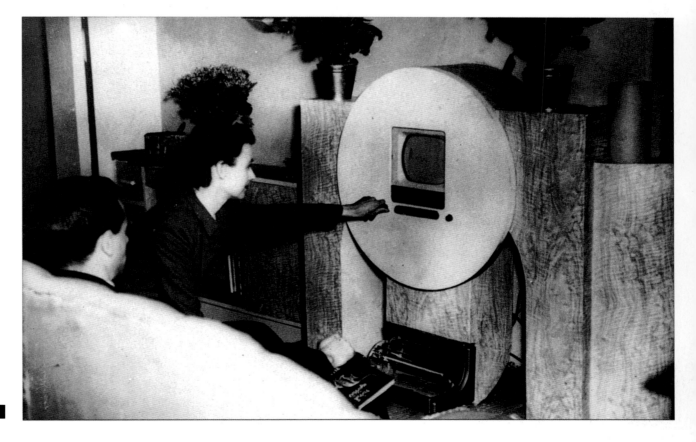

In 1948 Esquire magazine described the late forties styles in men's ties as the 'bold look'. The tie craze of the era carried through to the early fifties though as dress became more casual with open-necked shirts and T-shirts there was a steady decline in sales.

CHAPTER SIX
FASHION
AND
FANTASY

'ALL A DESIGNER CAN DO IS TO ANTICIPATE A MOOD BEFORE PEOPLE REALISE THAT
THEY ARE BORED WITH WHAT THEY HAVE ALREADY GOT. IT IS SIMPLY A QUESTION OF
WHO GETS BORED FIRST.'

MARY QUANT

INTRODUCTION

Within the decade virtually every extreme of fashion was seen. The fifties began with Dior's sheath and ended with De Bratzen's wide padded skirts and crinolines; the years between saw fashion take its image from sources as diverse as the Coronation of the Queen of England and the T-shirted, leather-jacketed Marlon Brando. It was the decade that saw the return of Chanel in 1954, and, a year later, the opening of a new chapter in fashion history with Mary Quant's Bazaar. And above all, it was the decade during which an entirely new movement appeared, teenage fashion.

Youth fashion had first become apparent in America of the forties with the bobby-soxer, but it was the fusion of fashion with other aspects of the age - rock-and-roll, a general image of rebellion and sometimes violence and the emergence of the teenager as a marketing target for films, records, cosmetics and so on - that made the fifties teen fashion a symbol of a whole lifestyle. It is this symbolism that seems to give the rocks-and-roll teenage fashion more power than it really had, for it was the next decade, in the wake of Mary Quant, that was to establish young design as a recognisable entity. But until then teenage fashion was derived from ready-made sources.

A NEW LOOK?

In the United States, the existing college clothes were mostly garish sports coats and windcheaters of cotton or one of the new man-made fibres. War surplus stores were a source of leather 'bomber' jackets, and hot-rodders customised T-shirts with club colours and insignia. Brando emerged from the cinema screen to demonstrate how impressionable young men, without the benefit of any training in method acting, could look mean and soulful in jeans and black leather. Britain, incidentally, missed out - *The Wild One* was banned there, although the French adopted the 'delinquent' look for its *blousons noirs*.

The advent of rock-and-roll brought to fashion the important essence of the music - the fusion of black and white - and the extrovert stage acts and dress-style of the black rhythm and blues musicians began to be an influence. Despite his poor rural background, Elvis Presley, for example, was wearing pink jackets and eye make-up before he had even cut his first disc! The white contribution to the rock-and-roll dress style was either Nashville/Country and Western, which mirrored the main ingredients in the mixture of music, or, later, the smart Italian look of the Fabian style of pop. Although the first generation of rock-and-rollers had developed their own image, commercialism soon resulted in image design; an obvious example was Elvis Presley's transformation

from country rocker to gold-lamé-suited superstar.

The most cynical packaging, however, was perpetrated by British impressario, Jack Good. Gene Vincent had a wild reputation; his record *Woman Love* had earned him a conviction for public lewdness and obscenity by the Virginia State Court and was banned by the BBC. Booking Vincent for a British TV show, Good was appalled to find him polite and neatly dressed. Vincent had been partially crippled in a motor-cycle accident and was in constant pain, but to create the effect he wanted, Good dressed him in tight black leather and designed a stage act that was physically painful to perform. On television, the compelling combination of rock-and-roll and anguish created a cult symbol for those rejecting the 'nice' image of the late-fifties pop star, and this extended to the early Beatles, who adopted the black leather look.

THE TEDDY BOY

The teenage style of the fifties that achieved the widest fame (or notoriety) occurred among England's working class. In the aftermath of the popularisation of Victorian and Edwardian style, which had been incorporated in the Festival of Britain, young officers of the Regiment of Guards, an upper class, elitist group, affected the Edwardian style for social wear. These Savile Row tailored garments featured long, high-necked jackets, sometimes of velvet, sometimes with velvet-trimmed collars and cuffs. In a further reaction against the general austerity of the time, the jackets were lined in either a floral print or bright red, further flamboyance being

1 **2**

1. So many aspects of the decade's style seem to be still with us as part of a fifties revival or simply because of their inherent quality, and it comes as a shock to see an image that makes the era remote. In 1950, when this picture was taken in London's Regent Street, the girdle incorporating suspenders was the key to the new, sleek look.

2. At a London dance hall, the men's neat suits could almost be a uniform. Apart from rock-and-roll fashion, clothes remained conservative, with 'smartness' and price the main considerations.

3. Sharply attired in Teddy boy style, with a velvet-collared and -cuffed jacket and narrow, 'drainpipe' trousers, the central figure stands out from his companions, who are conventionally dressed, working-class lads.

added by a brocade waistcoat. Against the common trend, the trousers were cut narrow, and the effect of extrovert eccentricity was enhanced by wing-collared shirts and sometimes suede shoes.

To appreciate fully the uniqueness of this mode of dress it should be remembered that at the time the British male ethos was of overt masculinity, and even suede shoes were regarded as the badge of the gay community - or of 'Nancy Boys' as the vernacular of the time had it. Furthermore, the drape jacket had styling echoes of those favoured by spivs (small-time gangsters and black marketeers), and those factors, combined with reports of wild living, gave the original Teddy Boys instant notoriety.

The newly emerged working-class teenagers, emancipated through their greatly increased wages and leisure, lacked suitable role models, and they were generally expected to dress much in the manner of their parents. Home dressmaking and knitting, which enjoyed a boom, enabled girls to customise existing fashions. But boys were either limited to cheap, off-the-peg stores, like the 'fifty shilling tailor' who offered a limited range of conventional styles, or they could resort to small, inexpensive tailors, which were then quite plentiful. Now that there was an identifiable style to emulate, working-class youths began to appear in the dance halls of South London in their Teddy Boy clothes. The originators, of course, soon dropped the style, which quickly became identified with rock-and-roll and violence (flick knives or switch blades and bicycle chains were standard dress accessories). Another essential accessory was the much-flaunted comb, which

1. Man-made fibres, were all part manifestations of the new Space Age technology; their novelty made them luxury goods.
2. Britain's post-war consumer shortages and rationing produced an increased interest in home dressmaking. Pictured in 1951, these window shoppers have an elegance that is an implicit advertising for the sewing-machine.

assumed symbolic significance; traditionally, the British working man had taken no interest in his hairstyle, generally being content with

the basic short back-and-sides. Now, the pompadour favoured by Little Richard and the DA, kept in place with Brylcreem, occupied the combs in constant motion. The male had become the peacock, while girls lacked the same inspiration (for there were no well-known female rock-and-roll singers and although Sandra Dee and Justine Corelli would later be role models, not even the most optimistic could attempt to emulate Marilyn Monroe) and rang the changes on a few basic styles.

MAN-MADE FASHION

The advent of man-made fibres had a conspicuous effect. In 1950, Dior had introduced a look that was the direct result of these textiles, for the sheath depended on the new elasticated-nylon roll-on girdles, which replaced the heavier, boned corsets and allowed a figure-hugging profile, especially as the roll-on incorporated stocking suspenders, thus doing away with the suspender belt. Tight, tailored skirts were 'smart', but for maximum effect on the dance floor the favoured look consisted of a wide, sometimes layered, skirt over several strata of petticoat, the waistline emphasised by a wide belt with a prominent buckle. Nylon blouses were topped with short, bolero-style jackets or with cardigans of angora wool. If there was 'electricity in the air' around one of these young ladies, it was most likely the static generated by all that nylon! For less strenuous

activities, such as hanging around coffee bars, the standard wear was tight toreador pants, either black or pastel shades, or pedal pushers, usually in pastel colours. There was, too, a type of colour coding, for under the influence of the Paris Left Bank image and the American beat look, black tended to denote seriousness and sophistication, and a real (or affected) interest in modern jazz, art films and existentialist philosophy.

Make-up favoured a black-eyed, pale-lipped look. Jewellery was either heavy wooden beads or 'craft' items made of copper and enamel, with heavy hoop earrings and bracelets. The men favoured either short hair that was brushed forward, or a shaggy, crudely cut style that was sometimes accompanied by a beard. Rough, textured clothing or corduroy garments and desert boots or sandals were the norm. In extremes, the beat look became unisex. Heavy knitted pullovers or artists' or fisherman's smocks became the uniform of anti-establishment and anti-pop. Folksy clothes showed that their wearers not only rejected contemporary fashion but also the 'artificial' nature of man-made fibres.

But synthetics are central to fifties fashion. For women, they revolutionised foundation garments, which, now less bulky, allowed, for example, the sheath look. Synthetics and plastics allowed, too, for better quality yet cheaper clothing, fresher colours and, in line with the general image of less domestic drudgery, permitted easier cleaning and care. Hitherto expensive materials, silk, lace, mohair, could be simulated, while the new vinyl plastics allowed imitation reptile skin, or glacé kid or even transparent Cinderella shoes, which enjoyed a brief heyday. The acceptance of the artificial, paralleled in the increased use of plastic generally, had a liberating effect. New, fluorescent colours began to be used, and cosmetic manufacturers, freed of any restrictions imposed by nature, produced lipsticks from near-white to near-purple and eye shadows in greens and blues. Nail varnish was now available in such a variety of colours that manufacturers were advocating a change several times a day to match the mood of the moment.

The hand, with elegant, varnished nails, became a major symbol in fifties advertising. It was a manifestation of how women were, at least in theory, freed from dirty domestic chores by the new technology. Everything, from aerosol dessert toppings to cars, waited at the push of a button and was finger-tip controlled! This new elegance was reflected in fashion, where there was new relation between 'high' and 'middle'. The early fifties saw a revival in prints, which, led by Pucci in 1950, were soon seen everywhere. Life ran a feature on the success of the English cotton firm, Horrocks, which was particularly popular in America. The newly emerging US fashion scene was willing to accept European style but was no longer prepared to be dictated to, and

American women demanded that fashion should reflect a more active lifestyle. By 1952 American *Vogue* was commenting: 'We want skirts we can step out of an automobile in without splitting their sides, sleeves, that reach for a telephone without straining their shoulders.'

By then America was influencing European style. The advances in knowledge of synthetics and the treatment of fabric were seen in raincoats, which no longer had to be rubberised and could therefore be smartly styled, and in swimwear. In 1951 *Vogue* reported that jeans were now chic for leisure wear. Costume jewellery, which had been growing in popularity throughout the forties, became an important feature, partly because of advanced American plastic technology, which included the plating of plastic for items such as radio knobs. Dior in particular favoured costume jewellery, and the style was endorsed by Mamie Eisenhower, who demonstrated that it was socially acceptable for even important occasions.

The year after Eisenhower's election, when the First Lady had worn Trifari jewels at the inaugural ball, the world was treated to a show of the real thing at the Coronation of Queen Elizabeth II. London suddenly became the centre of fashion, with Norman Hartnell, the designer of the Coronation gown, basing his own collection on the gold and white coronation colours. But the influence of pomp and ceremony was short lived, and indeed the dominance of *haute couture* in an age of mass consumerism was about to be challenged, first by Chanel in 1954, and in 1955 by Mary Quant.

THE END OF HAUTE COUTURE

Chanel had closed her legendary couture house in 1939, although the name had been kept alive in a perfume. Her return to fashion in 1954 re-introduced an earlier concept of deceptively simple clothes that were suitable for the smart working woman. Although not designed for mass production, Chanel's clothes could be easily copied, and by the late fifties, acknowledging that the pirating of her designs was commonplace, Chanel licensed Jeffrey Wallis in England to produce from her collections.

At the same time, similarly recognising a need for designed, but affordable and practical fashion, Mary Quant came onto the scene, opening Bazaar in Chelsea in 1955. Unlike Chanel, Quant was catering for a youthful market, for people in their late teens and early twenties, for whom, apart from the street fashion of rock-and-rollers or coffee bar beatniks, no identifiable style existed. Britain was still a class divided society. Although emotionally subscribing to the live-fast-die-young philosophy, working-class teenagers spent their short spells of youth in the knowledge that their lives would not end romantically, or dramatically like James Dean, nor perhaps through that fifties sword of Damocles,

the Bomb, but, with relentless certainty, with the draft into National Service for the boys and household chores for the girls. Nobody really expected anyone except the rich to have style, or, as it was significantly described, 'class'. But even the middle- and upper-class young had been ignored. With the exception of a few who adopted the Beat or Art School looks, which even Vogue recognised, they too suffered from adult-dominated fashion.

As early as 1953, *Vogue* had, under the influence of American *Vogue,* introduced a Young Idea section, but it featured nothing that was uniquely youth orientated. The gap became even more noticeable as increased travel opportunities and the spread of television made Britain aware of other lifestyles. Mary Quant's early styles relied on clean-cut, 1920s or 1930s styles or on shift-derived shapes (which were adopted by Paris), and they had a profound effect on the mass market from the end of the fifties.

Although, like Mary Quant, it is more closely associated with the sixties, Carnaby Street also came into being. John Stephen opened his first shop there in 1957, introducing the Italian style of male clothing. By then, Italian design had come to stand for modern, clean lines that, unlike Scandinavian modern, were chic and ever-so-slightly off-beat and typified by Espresso coffee machines and motor scooters. The clothes were sharply styled, with both jackets and trousers cut narrow and made usually of a lightweight fibre-mix fabric and complemented by a Perry Como hairstyle, and they symbolised, as did Quant, the new youth who neither conformed nor conspicuously rebelled. In 1959 Quant made a successful visit to America, where *Life* heralded her as the new fashion phenomenon. By then the first euphoria of rock-and-roll was over, Elvis was in the army, and America was becoming Europeanised. It was the end of an era.

3. Synthetic fabrics, combined with better print technology, allowed a profusion of leisure-wear styles to appear.

3

INFLUENCES

1. Although the high collar was favoured briefly by the young Guards officers who were the first 'teddy boys', it was the long waisted jacket and narrow trousers of the original Edwardian look that were the characteristics of Britain's first true youth fashion.

2. The influence of black fashion spread in the wake of music and dance. The zoot suit in this late 1930s picture of Harlem's Savoy ballroom became the uniform of the 'jitterbug'. Bop music and jive talk came to Europe via American servicemen.

5

3

4

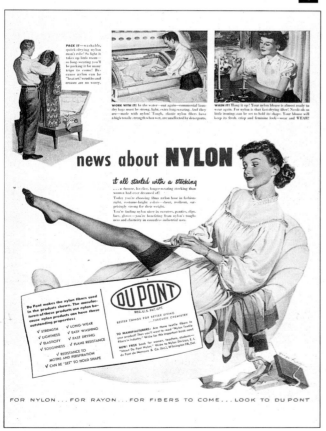

3. *Another main ingredient in the mixture that became rock-and-roll was Country and Western swing (Bill Haley) or rock-a-billy (Elvis Presley, Carl Perkins). Similarly the Nashville look, worn here by the Maddox Brothers and Rose contributed to rock-and-roll fashion.*

4. *'Nylons' became the universal name for stockings, which had hitherto been luxury items made of silk. Synthetic fabrics combined with the increased availability of consumer goods and higher earnings to raise living standards.*

5. *Man-made fibres became a major fashion influence. Clothes could be produced more economically and were easier to keep looking smart. Du Pont, who introduced the polyester 'Dacron' in the early fifties, demonstrated its qualities by putting the suit through a shower, then a washing machine, followed by an immersion in a swimming pool before it was finally worn for sixty-seven days without pressing!*

BLUE SUEDE SHOES ETC.

1

2

1. Early teenage fashion had little to distinguish it from adult clothing, although the availability of cheap printed cottons and man-made fibres made higher standards of dress possible for working girls.

2. New York teenagers in 1955 modelling different ways of using the latest fashion craze, headscarves. By later standards girls' clothes are conservative.

3. Fans seeking the autograph of singer Tommy Steele belie our image of retro rock-and-roll style. This casual dress is typical. High-necked or turtleneck sweaters were popular for girls, and the more stylish wear full-circle skirts.

3

4. Only the open-necked shirt and absence of a 'slim Jim' or bootlace tie mars this otherwise classic study of a 1955 British Teddy boy, with his brocade waistcoat (vest) and velvet-collared and -cuffed long, Edwardian-cut jacket.

5. The spectacular, uninhibited energy of the jive was the perfect expression of teenage liberation. The Saturday night hop gave dance virtuosos an opportunity to display their skills, the girls' wide skirts flaring up to echo Marilyn Monroe's famous pose.

BLUE JEAN BOP

1. 1952 New York teenagers wearing turned-up jeans. The hankies and screwed-up faces are a tribute to their idol Johnnie Ray, whose massive hit record Cry received extra publicity through Ray's ability to produce real tears on stage.

2. Though nothing else came close to the popularity of Davy Crockett hats, the popularity of all the western films made the cowboy look popular for children's clothes, such as this fringed, buckskin-style jacket.

3. Increased leisure time and the greater popularity of outdoor activities led to the adoption of the western look for casual wear.

4. The cowboy-style scarf became a feature of fifties dress, either in the obvious western manner shown here or in a more formal style.

5. By 1957, when this photo caught a demonstration of Italian rock-and-rollers, the jeans and checked shirt that represented the country from which rock-and-roll had, in part, originated, was about to be replaced by a slicker, more stylish fashion.

151

HAIR STYLING

1. Although the 'DA' hairstyle was politely known as the 'duck's tail', the initials obviously stand for another aspect of the bird's anatomy. Young men now had the money to spend on expensive hairstyling, a transitory symbol of freedom, for their hair would soon be shorn during a period of compulsory national service.

2. As well as the 'DA', there were other, more exotic variations - the bop, be-bop, teevee, panama, beechy head, dupe, back sweep and crest. The newly affluent young could spend on a haircut what their fathers might have considered a weekly wage.

3

4

5

3. Raymond - known as Mr Teasy-Weasy - was the top London hairdresser, and he introduced a variety of inventive styles. With what now seems period affectation, his staff adopted French names and pseudo-French accents.

4. Lustre Creme Shampoo, advertised as a favourite of Hollywood stars, was typical of the growing market for cosmetic and beauty products.

5. The continental-style gamine haircut and black sweater - went with record bars, modern jazz and 'art' cinema. As it is, the caption to this 1958 picture states that she's listening to one of her favourites - Pat Boone!

LIPSTICK, POWDER AND PAINT

1. What fun for your fingertips! Eight new Frosted 'Bon Bon' colors... so delicate...so feminine...in such good taste. Match them (as they do on the Riviera) to your gowns, your jewels—or contrast them! It's the chic new way to look—surprisingly subtle...but ooh la la!

C'est si bon?
...Mais non!

C'est les
'Bon Bons'
de *Revlon*

Delicious New Pastel Colors...
in 'Frosted Finger-Tints' for Summer
Très Chic!   Très Magnifique!

'BON BON'
nail enamels
○ PINEAPPLE YUM YUM   ○ PISTACHIO MINT
○ CHAMPAGNE TAFFY   ○ BUTTER PECAN
○ VIOLET CREME   ○ SUGAR BLUE
○ PINK COCONUT   ○ PLATINUM
(Taste one...taste four...taste them all)

2. BRONZE ANGEL...glorious sun-kissed shade of Angel Face by Pond's

Now in a smart, slim, new MIRROR CASE

Bronze Angel—the suntan you tuck in your handbag!

3. the brightest jewel of all can be your lips...

Tangee PRESENTS
"BRIGHT 'N CLEAR"
a new shade...a true shade...a just-right-for-you shade!

1. The American cosmetic firm Revlon used the background of Notre Dame, a poodle and champagne to emphasise the European influence of the new pastel look.

2. Suntan face powder is evidence of the increasing use of cosmetics during a period when manufacturers were counselling a 'look' for every occasion, including several complete changes during the course of each day!

3. During the first half of the decade, lipsticks were bright red, which, combined with Trifari-style earrings, produced the 'smart' American image.

4. Until European influence brought softer colours and a more natural look, cosmetics were used to produce a smart but essentially 'made-up' appearance.

5. Seated behind her pastel-coloured cosmetic pots, she makes up with what is an essentially artificial, if bright, look. Pink - on her face, in her housecoat, in her jars and ornaments - was the decade's favourite colour. Images such as this, of home, daily life and married bliss, filled advertisements and magazine editorial and were central to the way people saw themselves.

LEISURE WEAR

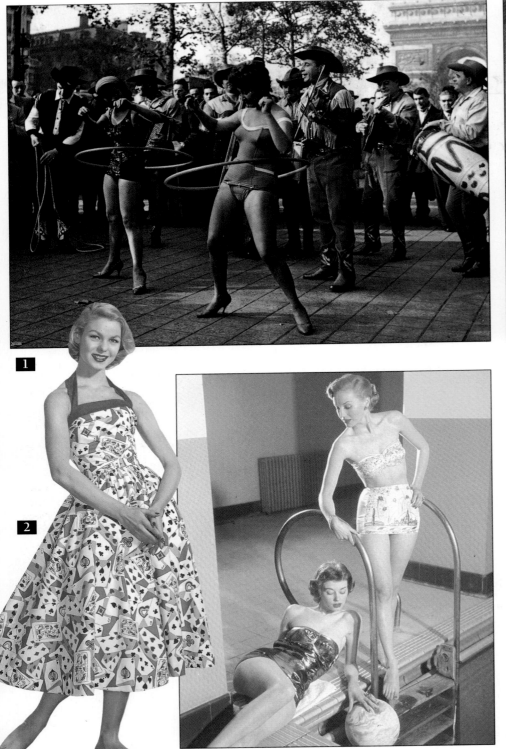

1. When the hula-hoop craze hit Paris, this demonstration, accompanied by a country-and-western band, stopped the traffic on the Champs-Elysées. In a decade in which fads and crazes proliferated, hula-hoops enjoyed phenomenal success, with competitions drawing entries from toddlers through to grannies.

3. The 1951 Festival of Britain inspired Festival motifs on almost everything. The two-piece bathing costume now seems demure compared with the abbreviated bikini that became popular within a few years.

2. By 1957, cotton was enjoying a revival after the first wave of popularity for synthetic fabrics, particularly as it was now treated in a way that allowed for ease of care. This particular pattern may have been influenced by Piero Fornasetti's prints of playing cards.

4. In 1950, even leisure wear was relatively formal in Britain. The casual American look of jeans or slacks filtered down from the top end of British fashion, having been championed by Vogue. The concept of 'street fashion' was in the future.

5

7

8

6

5. Chorus girls, trying out for the Jackie Gleeson show in 1954, wear virtually every style of beachwear. The woman in the front row has a particularly stylish 'continental' look - a matelot-striped strapless top, 'gypsy' hoop earrings and ankle bracelet.

6. Looking like an adman's dream, an American family set off for a picnic. Although his business clothes would still have been conservative, in his leisure time the man could enjoy wearing a flamboyant sports shirt. Note the radio - within a few years the transistor reduced the portable radio to pocket size.

7. Although this 1954 outfit was French-designed, it is essentially American in style, with moccasins, turned-up pants and soft knitwear. The chunky costume jewellery bracelet is also typically American.

8. Despite the shorts and open shirt, this 1953 picture of Zena Marshall shows the formal make-up that characterised the early fifties. By the end of the decade, cosmetic companies, influenced by the growing youth market, were bringing out softer colours and encouraging a more 'natural' look of make-up.

DRIP DRY GENERATION

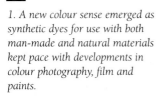

1. A new colour sense emerged as synthetic dyes for use with both man-made and natural materials kept pace with developments in colour photography, film and paints.

2. The increased durability and ease of care of everyday wear were the most notable effects of the introduction of synthetic fibres, but they also enabled special clothing, such as bridal gowns, to be manufactured economically.

3. In an age that, naïvely, believed that 'new' automatically meant 'better', the material was promoted as much as the product.

4

'TERYLENE' AND THE MODERN WOMAN

6

5

4. The American company Du Pont made major contributions to the development of synthetic fibres. Here, scientists are seen at work on early experiments.

5. Populuxe style allowed men's leisure clothing to become less conservative. This scene, from the French poodle and pink shirt to the Vegas hat and blue suede shoes, encapsulates the essence of the period.

6. The most popular feature of synthetic fibres was the fact that they could be made to simulate traditional fabrics. Genuine cotton moved up market, and the industry declined, as its role was taken over by man-made substitutes, which, superficially at least, replicated the real thing.

KITSCH FASHION

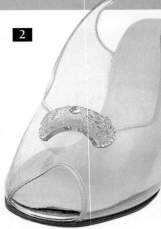

1. Whether adopting a space theme or the Mexican look, the decade that produced a stream of crazes and fads found ephemeral fashions to match.

2. Plastics technology was readily accepted in fashion, and man-made fabrics symbolised progress. Transparent shoes, known as Cinderella slippers, enjoyed a vogue, despite being rather uncomfortable.

3. The trellis pattern, seen in this American plastic handbag, was a popular motif.

7. Almost pop-art objects in their own right, these gold-metal-flake sun-glasses typify an age of glitter.

4. The vogue for costume jewellery made it acceptable for even expensive items to be made of plastic, as with this American handbag.

5. More a novelty than a true fashion accessory, these sun-glasses were popularly known as 'sin glasses'.

6. The transparent heels of these American Cinderella slippers are embedded with diamante; they were known as 'follow me heels'.

FILM STAR LOOK

1. Although critics were generally antagonistic and derided her ambitions to be recognised as a serious actress, Marilyn Monroe's image dominates the decade - whether it is of her early days as a Playboy centrefold, or when she entertained troops in Korea, or as the fantasy ingénue of The Seven Year Itch. Her legend continues to grow: she seems as much the centre of media attention as ever.

2. James Dean symbolised the cult of youthful rebellion. Even his death in a car crash in 1955, two weeks before Rebel without a Cause went on release, accorded with his intense image. During his brief film career he was highly regarded as an actor, and he can be remembered as much for this as for his glamour.

3. Doris Day starred in musicals and even a Hitchcock thriller, The Man Who Knew Too Much (1956), before finding her niche as the all-American girl-next-door in Pillow Talk (1959), the first of several light comedies.

4

4. Belgian-born Audrey Hepburn, seen here with Fred Astaire in Funny Face (1956), had an air of European chic, described by Vogue as being 'a new kind of beauty'. She was unlike the typical Hollywood star, very much in the Vogue image, and was usually dressed by the French couturier de Givenchy, who had provided her wardrobe for Sabrina (1954) and supplied the numerous creations she wore in Funny Face.

5. A star of Singin' in the Rain (1952) and The Tender Trap (1955), Debbie Reynolds dominated the fanzine gossip magazines in 1958 when she lost her husband, singer Eddie Fisher, to Elizabeth Taylor. This 1954 photo, showing Debbie in shorts and a tight sweater, is typical of the publicity material of the time.

3

5

SOPHISTICATES

1. A stunning display of mid-fifties opulence is shown in this 1955 group photo of designers and their models.

2. An evening dress by Pierre Balmain from his 1953 winter collection. The long, close-fitting sheath-type dress was the main Paris look for that season.

3. *Vogue* model Barbara Goalen, one of the famous faces of the fifties, models Mattli's Petunia evening dress. In 1953, the year of this picture, models still adopted a rather posed stance.

4. French poodles and opera gloves were the chic accessories for this 1951 French-cut outfit.

5. Lattice enjoyed a vogue as a design motif, and chiffon, which had been mainly a milliner's fabric, was applied in new ways.

JEWELLERY

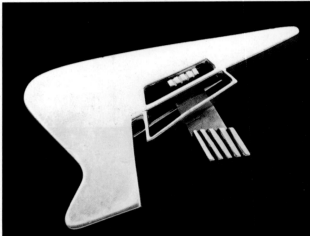

1. Costume jewellery dominated both high and low fashion. Here the coins are British but the jewellery is American.

2. A futuristic silver and gold brooch by American designer Margaret Da Patta.

3. Forties gilt bracelet and brooch by the American designer Kreisler anticipating the costume jewellery of the fifties.

4

. A 'flying saucers' powder
ompact by Kico, now regarded
s a classic.

. The vogue for costume
ewellery did not entirely usurp
he real thing. These items are by
he French firms of Van Cleef and
rpels.

6. High-quality plastic jewellery,
such as this American-made
Scottie dog brooch, soon found
cheap imitators.

7. So fashionable was the
costume jewellery made by the
American firm Trifari, that First
Lady Mamie Eisenhower wore
Trifari for the presidential
inauguration ball. This brooch
dates from 1950.

6

5

7

Maschera *by painter and illustrator, Ben Shahn, 1959.*

CHAPTER SEVEN

THIS IS TOMORROW

'FRIED SHOES. LIKE IT MEANS NOTHING, DON'T SHOOT THE WARTHOG.'

GEOGORY CORSO, BEAT POET

INTRODUCTION

After World War II the nucleus of modern art shifted dramatically from Paris to New York. Fernand Léger, Max Ernst, Piet Mondrian, André Masson and, later, Salvador Dali, among others, had moved in from Europe, but this phenomenon was, unlike the contemporary developments in architecture, not led by Europeans but by an American, Jackson Pollock.

ABSTRACT EXPRESSIONISM

Pollock himself dismissed the concept of national style as 'absurd...just as the idea of a purely American mathematics or physics would seem absurd...the basic problems of comtemporary painting are independent of any country.' Nevertheless, the prominence in the arts achieved by New York, not only in architecture and painting but also in the performing arts, with the founding of the New York City Ballet under Georges Balanchine, the development of theatre with the school of method acting, and modern jazz, seems to coincide with the rise of the United States to the principle power in the West.

Although its origins lay in surrealism, abstract expressionism, particularly action painting, avoids even subconscious imagery - the artist allows him-or herself to be directed by the painting. Pollock was the main exponent of action painting and certainly its most famous practitioner, for his work attracted much press attention, including an article in *Time,* which called him 'Jack the Dripper'. He rejected the parameters of a pre-stretched canvas, but, laying a large area of the material on the floor, applied paint, including sign writer's enamel, and sometimes sand or other materials by dribbling and splashing it on, and manipulating it with sticks, knives and so on until he had finished. The 'action' was not only the application of the media but also Pollock's constant movement round and over the work, which he described as being 'in' his painting. 'When I am in my painting, I'm not aware of what I'm doing. It is only after a sort of 'acquainted' period that I see what I have been about. I have no fears about making changes, destroying the image, etc. because the painting has a life of its own. I try to let it come through. It is only when I lose contact with the

1. Sam Francis moved to Paris in 1950, having previously studied medicine in the United States. His work, though obviously closely connected to the American School of Abstract Expressionism, is of the European style known as Tachisme, where the finished painting fixes the energy which was used in making it, with splatters and paint runs left as evidence.

most unique contribution was made by Helen Frankenthaler, who introduced properties of light into her work through the use of translucent 'stain' paints. This effect of thin paint can also be seen in the work of Sam Francis, but the more general image of paint in abstract expressionist painting was thick and tactile.

Action painting was only a manifestation of a broader school of abstract expressionism, the physical nature of which sometimes gave the impression that it was anti-intellectual. The fallacy of this is illustrated in the work of Robert Motherwell, who had published a history of the Dada movement and who is best known for a series of pictures, *Elegies to the Spanish Republic* (1955-60), which has a quality of monumental stillness, rather than the drips and splashes of energetically applied paint. In contrast, another abstract expressionist, Willem de Kooning, was not really 'abstract', in the sense that such works as *Woman and bicycle* (1952-3) are discernible images.

Abstract expression continued to be the dominant style in America, although its significance waned after (but not as a result of) Pollock's death. In Europe a figurative painting prevailed. However, in his final years, Henri Matisse produced some of the purest abstract work when he abandoned paint in favour of coloured paper. The *papier decoupé* technique, which enabled him to work on a scale that he was physically too weak otherwise to tackle, can be seen as the epitome of the post-painterly abstracts of the sixties. Of the older generation, only Matisse succeeded in this degree of innovation, although Miró, too, continued to develop in a way that was relevant to the time. Picasso came to be regarded as an anachronism, his fifties series of re-workings of famous paintings of the past appearing often mannered and artificial.

KITCHEN-SINK ART

England saw a major revival of figurative painting. Graham Sutherland produced portraits, so bringing his art closer to the expectations of the public. However, the mid-fifties also saw the emergence of social-realism in the kitchen-sink school. This was essentially literary art, which took as its sources both the painterly qualities of David Bomberg and the literary, socialist influence of the generation of angry young men. Though fashionable at the time, the kitchen-sink style, of which the main exponent was John Bratby, had a parochial and self-conscious negative limitation of subject and technique, which mercifully inhibited its continuance. In any event, the superficial shock of the kitchen-sink school was overshadowed by the work of Francis Bacon, which though figurative, shares with the Kooning the area that, were it not for the inherent contradiction, might best be described as 'figurative-abstract-expressionism'. This can most clearly be explained in Bacon's own words: 'I think that you can make, very much as in abstract painting,

painting that the result is a mess. Otherwise there is a pure harmony, an easy give and take, and the painting comes out well.' The concept of the canvas as a sort of ouija board, whereby a bond exists between it and the artist during the painting process, was not absolute, for Pollock frequently trimmed his paintings down afterwards to a 'picture' area. Pollock was killed in a car crash in 1956, aged 44, sharing with James Dean the fifties image of a transitory star. His own description of his work likewise has a period, almost beat-poet-like quality: 'It's just like a bed of flowers. You don't have to tear your hair out over what it means.'

Unfortunately overshadowed by their husbands, Lee Krasner, wife of Pollock, and Elaine de Kooning were talented abstract expressionist painters, and other notable women painters in the genre were Grace Hartigan, Joan Mitchell and Helen Frankenthaler. It is worth remembering in the context of the macho image of this particular art form that so many exponents were women. Of the above, the

2. David Bomberg, whose 1956 Self portrait is seen here, represents the continuing tradition of Expressionism. By the 1950s this school seemed rather old-fashioned but it remained an influence in painting technique.

involuntary marks on the can
vas which may suggest much deeper ways by which you can
trap the facts you are obsessed by: If anything ever does
work in my case it works from that moment when
consciously I didn't know what I was doing.'

THE NEW REALISM

While the relationship between conscious and unconscious
control was being explored by painters whose work was as
dissimilar as that of Pollock and of Bacon, a European
movement, sometimes called New Realism, began to appear
towards the end of the decade. Anticipating the 'happenings'
of the sixties, Yves Klein staged events during which nude
girls, covered in paint, flung themselves onto a canvas-
covered floor, while in the background musicians performed
his *Monotone Symphony* (10 minutes of a single sustained
note). In Paris in 1958 Klein exhibited an empty, white-
painted gallery, and other conceptual work included
paintings mutated through a flame thrower or washed by the
rain. A contemporary of Klein, Christo began the 'packaged'
buildings, a form that is still being carried out.

POP ART

Yet another form and one that leads directly into a major
style of the sixties is pop art. With its roots in Dada and
surrealism, pop began to be seen as an identifiable school in
the mid-fifties. As with any other style, its parameters are
hard to define. British artist Eduardo Paolozzi, for example,
in *I was a Rich Man's Plaything* (1947), anticipates the
common vocabulary of pop. For a start, the title is taken
from the contents of *Intimate Confessions,* a magazine whose
front cover, complete with pin-up, dominates the top half of
the picture. The visual pun, another element, is included
with the picture of a hand holding a bottle-shaped gun, from
the mouth/muzzle of which comes a balloon with the
cartoon-lettered word *Pop.* Below the magazine cover
appears another element, the icon in the form of a postcard
of an American Flying Fortress bomber, and a Coca-Cola
bottle and sign. Another early appearance of pop was
Barbara Jones's 'Black Eyes and Lemonade' Exhibition at the
Whitechapel Art Gallery, part of the 1951 Festival of Britain,
which contained, among examples of Victorian kitsch, a
1930s suburban-type tiled fireplace in the shape of an
Airedale dog.

The emergence of pop in Britain was due in part to the
ambivalent attitude that the young artists of the time felt
towards Americanism. The pop/consumerist culture was
experienced vicariously during the war and in the immediate
post-war period, and it coincided with an intellectual and an
emotional rejection of the Establishment. In this
environment, a splinter group from the Institution of
Contemporary Arts, the Independent Group, which was
formed in 1952, was breaking new ground in seriously

examining the implications of this alternative culture. The
first meeting of the group was at a seminar in which Paolozzi
produced for discussion such items as *Amazing Science
Fiction* magazines, and American car and food
advertisements. These images, it was proposed, would be the
vocabulary of the new art, which Paolozzi's mentor, Jean
Dubuffet, whom he had met in Paris in the late forties, was
describing as *art brut.*

The idea of a new, post-war value of aesthetics was also
expounded by the architects Peter and Alison Smithson -
with the style known as New Brutalism. The Smithsons were
joint organisers with Paolozzi of the Independent Group's
'Parallel of Life and Art' Exhibition in 1953. The only 'art'
shown was a photograph of Pollock at work together with
photographs of work by Picasso, Klee and Dubuffet. The rest
of the exhibition consisted of photographs of images from

*1. Francis Bacon has described
his painting as capturing
emotion; its purpose is to 'make a
certain type of feeling visual'. His
painting often refers to images
from the work of earlier artists
(Vel zquez's portrait of Pope
Innocent X) or film (the
screaming nurse from Battleship
Potemkin) but the prime force
comes from a handling of paint
which is uncompromisingly
expressionist.*

technical and scientific studies, children's art and pictures of industry.

The painter Richard Hamilton, a member of the Independent Group, exhibited his work in 1955. The next year he designed an exhibition, 'Man, machine and motion', which examined the relationship between machine aesthetics and art. The culmination of the Independent Group was the 'This Is Tomorrow' exhibition at the Whitechapel Gallery in 1956, which included such 'pop' images as a 16-foot tall robot, a life-size picture of Marilyn Monroe and a jukebox playing in the background. The title of Hamilton's poster for the exhibition, *Just What is it that Makes Today's Homes so Different, so Appealing?* is (as had been Paolozzi's *I was a Rich Man's Plaything*) evocative of contemporary magazine articles. The montage is a humorous juxtaposition of a pin-up and a muscular body builder in a modern interior. His immediately subsequent work, *Hommage à Chrysler Corp* (1957), *Hers is a Lush Situation* (1958) and *She* (1958), were more subtle but no less a commentary on American consumer values. By now the images that Paolozzi, a pioneer of pop art, had seen purely as images, were being used by artists for their symbolism. Hamilton commented retrospectively that 'the worst thing that can happen to a girl, according to the ads, is that she should fail to be exquisitely at ease in her appliance setting - the setting that now does much to establish our attitude to a woman in the way that her clothes used to. Sex is everywhere, symbolised in the glamour of mass-produced luxury - the interplay of fleshy plastic and smooth, fleshier metal.'

American pop art, in contrast, was far closer to Dada, which Marcel Duchamp (who had claimed invention of the term) had introduced in his ready-mades so long ago. His *Bicycle Wheel* dates from 1913, and shortly after emigrating from Paris to New York he had exhibited *Fountain*, a urinal signed 'R. Mutt', in 1917. American pop art did not have the cultural duality that British artists such as Hamilton and Paolozzi brought to their work by the use of American imagery, although this was itself rejected by British artist Peter Blake, who, while referring to American pop icons such as Elvis, found his themes among folk art, such as fairground painting and seaside postcards. Despite the pop motifs, much of the major work, such as Japser Johns' 'flag' paintings, treat the subject matter as a neutral foundation for pure painting.

Similarly, de Kooning used the mouth of the girl in the Camel cigarette T-Zone advertisements - 'for taste and for my throat, Camels are tops in enjoyment!' - as the shape he wanted. The paintings themselves are not in any way linked with Camel cigarettes. A similar negation of image occurred in the work of Roy Lichtenstein, who said of the themes of comic illustration and commercial art: 'I accept it as being there, in the world. Signs and comic strips are interesting as

subject matter. There are certain things that are useable, forceful and vital about commercial art.' Although it is often assumed that Lichtenstein simply copied enlarged areas of existing commercial pictures, he explained: 'Artists have never worked with the model - just with the painting. My work is actually different from comic strips in that every mark is really in a different place, however slight the difference seems to some.'

Pop art, in the next decade, was to take on further strata of meaning with the artist, Andy Warhol, becoming a pop-cult figure and, significantly, using as an image Marilyn Monroe, the enduring fifties pop-cult figure.

2. Crammed with imagery from popular magazines, its title a parody of a magazine article, Hamilton's Just What is it That Makes Today's Homes so Different, so Appealing? *is almost a documentary record of the age. It marks the beginning of an aspect of pop art concerned with explicit social commentary.*

INFLUENCES

1. Le Port *by Joan Miró. The surrealists rejected the intellectual confines of the early twentieth-century movements. Cubism and Futurism, in favour of 'poetic' painting and so laid the foundation of abstract expressionism.*

2. Optical discs *by Marcel Duchamp (1935). Dada, which Duchamp claimed to have 'invented', was a form of surrealism. It was initially controversial because works incorporated real, found objects. Dada resurfaced in the late forties and through the fifties as pop art.*

3. Mondrian explored pure abstraction intellectually, clinically, by arranging space and mass on the canvas. By the end of the thirties it did not look as if this particular ascetic route through abstract painting could be pursued further and Mondrian's successors, the abstract expressionists, were free to add new dimensions of emotion and violence to their art. Illustrated is a 1937 composition.

4. Sonia Terk Delaunay was the creator of the Orphist movement, which was to emphasize colour and energy as the prime ingredients of painting. Her 1939 Rhythme Coloré is shown here. Together with her husband Robert, Delaunay has been credited with making major contributions, in earlier works, to the foundations of pure abstract art, the exploration of which dominated the fifties.

5. The American painter James Abbott McNeill Whistler, who lived in England, was profoundly influenced by Impressionism and Japanese art, as can be seen in Old Battersea Bridge: Nocturne-Blue and Gold (1865). The accusation by Ruskin that Whistler 'flung a pot of paint in the face of the public' was later echoed in adverse comments on the work of Jackson Pollock. Pollock was himself the heir to Impressionism's liberation of painting methods.

ABSTRACT EXPRESSIONISM

1. *Amorous Dance by Karel Appel (b.1921). Dutch-born Appel was a founder of the Cobra art group in Paris, where he worked from 1950, and a leading exponent of the 'dynamic' style of abstract expressionism.*

2. *Full Fathom Five by Jackson Pollock, who was described by Time as 'Jack the dripper'. He became the leading figure in abstract expressionism at a time when the United States appeared to be usurping Europe as the centre of modern art. By avoiding traditional painting techniques action painting sought to allow the artist's subconscious to manifest itself.*

3. *American pop art was initially less figurative and literary than the British school, and although Robert Rauschenberg (b.1925) is generally categorized as 'pop', in his 'combine' paintings (which incorporate objects) such as* The Red Painting *shown here, there is a large painterly element.*

POETRY IN MOTION

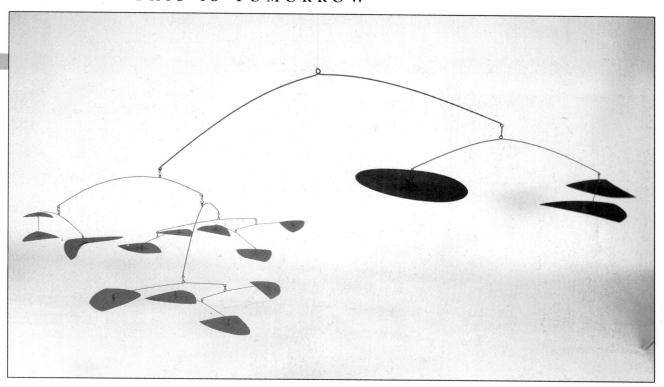

1. The UNESCO Offices in Paris, designed by Breuer, Zehrfuss and Nervi, is in fact three buildings, which, in addition to a Japanese garden by Noguchi, display examples of major modern art, including The Spiral by Alexander Calder. The same year as The Spiral, 1958, Calder also contributed to the Brussels Expo with Whirling Ear.

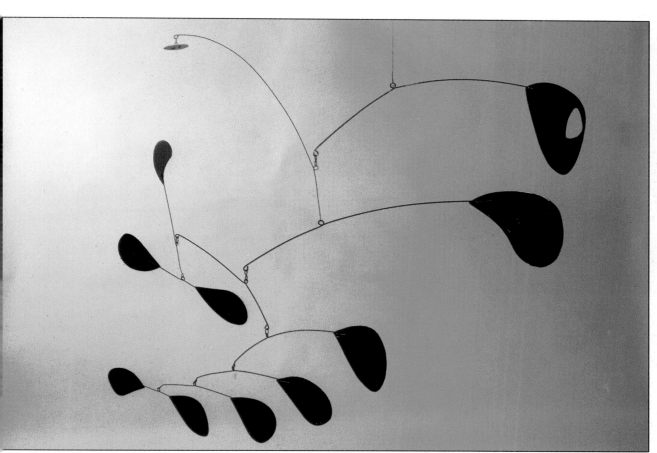

2. Blue Boomerang (1958) by Alexander Calder. He trained initially as an engineer, becoming known in the 1920s for his animated toy circus, from which he progressed to abstracts, which Marcel Duchamp termed mobiles, the genre for which Calder is best known, although he has also worked as a jeweller and illustrator.

3. Calder's influence permeates the fifties. It may be seen in the lighting of Serge Moule, the furniture of Harry Bertoia, in graphics and in architecture. Jean-Paul Sartre described one of Calder's mobiles as 'an object defined by its movement, which does not exist outside it, a flower which withers as soon as it is stopped'.

MURALS

1. Britain's traditions of public
art had been largely confined to
monumental statuary. During the
late forties and early fifties public
art of a different kind - the social
documentary art of Diego Rivera
- became more widely known.
There was a feeling that the post-
war years would be more
egalitarian, socially humane and
as a result figurative murals
began to be commissioned, such
as this example designed for a
sports centre in 1950.

2. A stylised, Rousseauesque
ceiling panel by John Reid, 1957,
incorporates pictorial images in a
decorative manner.

3. Industry contributed to the Festival of Britain. Seen here are the stylised lion and unicorn for ICI. Although some contemporary commentators derided the populist nature of the festival, it was in fact the intention that there should be a high content of whimsical, decorative elements such as this, in keeping with the theme 'A Tonic to the Nation'.

SCULPTURE

1. Henry Moore began to move away from the monumental literary style he had adopted in the fifties and undertook a series of abstract structures of which the components fitted together, a device that had already been used by Jean Arp in the thirties. This public sculpture on the Embankment in London is called Interlocking Forms.

2. Tree Forms as Mother and Child by Henry Moore. Despite a prolific output, Moore is remarkable for having absorbed the influences of other artists without contributing any great originality himself.

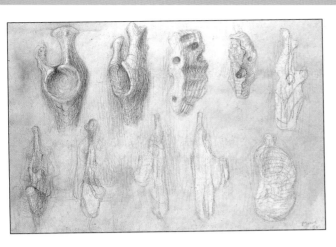

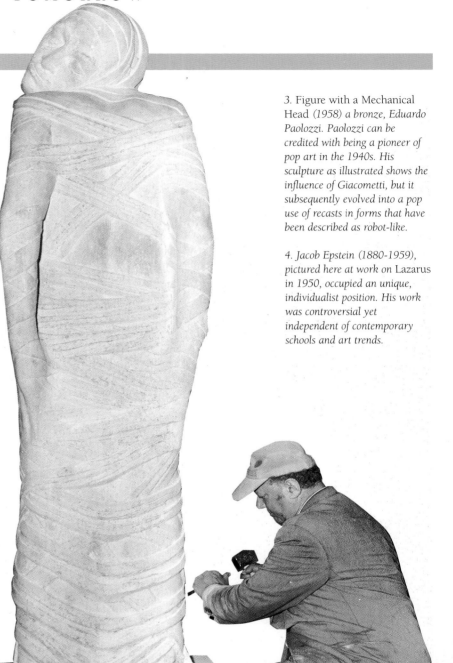

3. Figure with a Mechanical Head (1958) a bronze, Eduardo Paolozzi. Paolozzi can be credited with being a pioneer of pop art in the 1940s. His sculpture as illustrated shows the influence of Giacometti, but it subsequently evolved into a pop use of recasts in forms that have been described as robot-like.

4. Jacob Epstein (1880-1959), pictured here at work on Lazarus in 1950, occupied an unique, individualist position. His work was controversial yet independent of contemporary schools and art trends.

183

3. Before the Caves (1958) is a definitive example of Helen Frankenthaler's unique abstract expressionist painting. She was initially influenced by Jackson Pollock but abandoned the easel in favour of large unstretched, raw canvas (Before the Caves measures 9 x 9ft) and worked on the floor. The canvas was not primed allowing the thin, stain paint which characterised her work to soak into the fabric. The translucent properties of her painting influenced other painters, most particularly Morris Louis.

1. The influence of husband Willem on Elaine de Kooning's painting is undeniable. She had been his student, but within a short time both painters were regarded as equally important contributors to the 1940s New York abstract art scene. Elaine de Kooning was also a respected art critic and writer. In 1957 she took a teaching post at the University of New Mexico and produced a series of works based on bullfights, one of which, Sunday Afternoon is shown here.

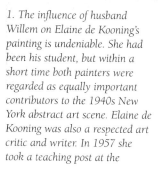

2. The Scottish artist Joan Eardley (1921-63) shows in Street Kids (early 1950s), a strong social realism in the manner of the kitchen sink school.

4. Landscape at Kyleakin (late 1950s) by Anne Redpath (1895-1965). A dominant 'painterly' approach is evident here, strongly influenced by Expressionism. This landscape, with its sombre ominous colours, is atypical; her painting more commonly used bright colour.

1. *Although the inclusion of graphic ready-mades was not a new idea (it was reminiscent of Kurt Schwitters' work in the 1920s) the 'decollage' (torn posters) of British artist Nigel Henderson's* Hoarding *(1951) is essentially pop. Henderson was a champion of New Brutalism and a founding member of the Independent Group, and* Hoarding *related to the reality of the fenced-off city landscape of bomb sites rather than to the whimsical gaiety of the Festival of Britain.*

2. *Peter Blake's* On the Balcony *(1955-7) is an illustrative icon of British pop culture. An 'I Love Elvis' badge and Union Jacks, a Lucky Strike cigarette pack and images of the Royal family, including Princess Margaret on the cover of* Life *magazine, encapsulate the essence of grass-roots pop culture.*

INDEX

INDEX

CREDITS

Quarto would like to thank the following for their help with this publication and for permission to reproduce copyright material.

pp2/3:©DACS
pp10/11: (1) Colin McArthur (2) Popperfoto
pp12/13: (2-3) Macdonald/Aldus Archive, (4) Herman Miller
pp14/15: (1) (4) EWA
pp16/17: (2) Popperfoto, (4) Topham
pp20/21: (1) Popperfoto
pp22/23: (1) Mcdonald/Aldus Archive
p24/25: (2) Raymond Loewy International Inc, (3) Architectural Association, (4) Macdonald/Aldus Archive
pp26/27: (2)(5)(6) Macdonald/Aldus Archive, (3) Quadrant Picture Library, (7) EWA
p28/29: (1)(3) Jaguar Cars, (2)(7) Macdonald/Aldus Archive (4)(5) Popperfoto, (6) Hulton-Deutsch Collection
pp30/31: (5)(6) Macdonald/Aldus Archive, (7) Textron's Bell Aerospace Division, Buffalo, NY
pp34/35: (1) Hulton-Deutsch Collection, (5) Popperfoto
p36/37: (1)(3) Hulton-Deutsch Collection, (2)(5)(6) Popperfoto
pp38: (1)(3) Hulton-Deutsch Collection, (2)(4) Popperfoto
p42/43: (2)(3) The Kobal Collection, (4) Popperfoto
p44/45: (1) Popperfoto
pp46/47: (1) Hulton-Deutsch Collection, (2) Macdonald/Aldus Archive, (3) National Film Archive, London, (4) Colin McArthur, (5) Dat's Jazz/Max Jones
pp48/49: (1-5) The Kobal Collection
p50/51: (1)(2)(3)(5) The Kobal Collection, (4) Jean-Loup Charmet
p52/53: (1-5) The Kobal Collection
pp54/55: (1)(3-6) The Kobal Collection, (2) National Film Archive, London

p56/57: (1-5)(7) The Kobal Collection
p58/59: (2)(5) The Kobal Collection, (3) (4) (6) National Film Archive, London
p60/61: (1)(6)(7)(8) Macdonald/Aldus Archive, (2)(3)(4)(5) Popperfoto
p62/63: (1)(2)(3) Popperfoto
p64/65: (1) The Kobal Collection, (2) National Film Archive, London, (3) (4) Colin McArthur
p66/67: (1) MCA Records, (3) The Kobal Collection, (4)(5) Popperfoto
pp70/71: (1) Angelo Hornak Photographic Library (2) Architectural Association
pp72/73: (1) Architectural Association
pp74/75: (2-3)(4)(6) Architectural Association, (5) Macdonald/Aldus Archive
pp76/77: (1) Popperfoto, (2)(6)(7) Architectural Association, (3) (5) Hulton-Deutsch Collection, (4) Macdonald/Aldus Archive
pp78/79: (1) Popperfoto
pp80/81: (1-3) Angelo Hornak Photographic Library, (4-6) Architectural Association
pp82/83: (1)(3)(4)(5)(7) Architectural Association, (6) Angelo Hornak Photographic Library
pp84/85: (1) Jean-Loup Charmet, (2) The Architectural Press, (3) Royal Institute of British Architecture
pp86/87: (2) Popperfoto, (3) Macdonald/Aldus Archive, (4) EWA, (5) Architectural Association
pp90/91: (1) The Kobal Collection, (2) Architectural Association
pp94/95: (1)(2)(4)(5) Macdonald/Aldus Archive, (6)©DACS 1989
pp96/97: (2)(3)(6)(8) The Robert/Opie Collection
pp98/99: (1)(3)(4) EWA, (5) Popperfoto, (2) Moira Clinch, (6) Hulton-Deutsch Collection, (7) J. Allan Cash

pp100/101: (1) Architectural Association, (2) Popperfoto
pp104/105: (1) Jean-Loup Charmet
pp106/107: (2)(3) Macdonald/Aldus Archive, (4)(5)(6) Jean-Loup Charmet
pp108/109: (4) Architectural Association
pp110/111; (3) The Kobal Collection
p114/115: (1) EWA, (2) Hulton-Deutsch Collection, (3) Jean-Loup Charmet, (4) Cobra and Bellamy
pp116/117: (2) Popperfoto, (3) EWA
pp118/119: (1)(4) Macdonald/Aldus Archive, (2)©COSMOPRESS, Geneva & DACS, London 1989, (3) Colin McArthur, (5) Japanese Information Centre, London
pp120/121: (1)(4) Macdonald/Aldus Archive, (2)(5) Christies
pp122/123: (1) Hulton-Deutsch Collection, (3) Popperfoto
pp124/125:(1) EMI, (4) (5) Popperfoto
pp126/127: (1)(4) Cobra and Bellamy, (2)(5) Macdonald/Aldus Archive
pp130/131: (1) (2) EWA, (3) Heals April '52', (4) Macdonald/Aldus Archive
pp132/133: (1) Popperfoto
pp134/135: (1) Macdonald/Aldus Archive, (6) EWA, (7) Cobra and Bellamy
pp136/137: (1) Angelo Hornak Photographic Library, (5) Rosenthal, (6) Poole Potteries, (7) Cobra and Bellamy
pp138/139: (4) (5) Architectural Association
pp142/143: (1)(2) Popperfoto, (3) Hulton-Deutsch Collection
pp146/147: (1) Hulton-Deutsch Collection, (2) The Bettmann Archive Inc, (3) Country Music Foundation Library and Media Center, (5) Macdonald/Aldus Archive
pp148/149: (1)(3)(5) Popperfoto, (2) Macdonald/Aldus Archive, (4)

Hulton-Deutsch Collection
pp150/151: (2) Macdonald/Aldus Archive, (5) Popperfoto
pp152/153: (1) (2) (5) Popperfoto, (3) Hulton-Deutsch Collection
pp154/155: (5) Popperfoto
pp156/157: (1-4) (6-8) Popperfoto, (5) Macdonald/Aldus Archive, (7) Hulton-Deutsch Collection
pp158/159: (4) Macdonald/Aldus Archive, (5) EWA, (6) ICI Fibres
pp162/163: (3-5) The Kobal Collection
pp164/165: (1)(3) Popperfoto, (2) Designers and Models, (5) Hulton-Deutsch Collection
pp166/167: (1) Popperfoto, (2)(3)(4)(6) Cobra and Bellamy
pp168/169©DACS 1989
pp172/173: (1) Marlborough Fine Art (London) Ltd
pp174/175: (1)(3)©DACS 1989, (2)(4)©ADAGP, Paris & DACS, London 1989
pp176/177: (2)(3)©DACS 1989
pp178/179: (1) Angelo Hornak Photographic Library, (2-3)©ADAGP, Paris, DACS, London 1989
pp180/181: (1-3) Royal Institute of British Architects
pp182/183: (1)(2) The works illustrated have been reproduced by kind permission of the Henry Moore Foundation, (3) Published by kind permission of the artist, (4) Popperfoto
pp184/185: (1) Collection Ciba-Geigy Corporation, (2)(4) National Gallery of Scotland, (3) Ben Blackwell

Every effort has been made to trace and acknowledge all copyright holders. Quarto would like to apologize if any omissions have been made.